Brick by Brick – Building Resilience in Chaos and Kindness by Being Resilient in Conflict and Kinship

Nicholle Vincent Brock

Copyright © 2025 Nicholle Vincent Brock

All rights reserved.

Written permission must be secured from the author to use or reproduce any part of this book. No part of this book can be stored in a retrieval system of any sort nor transmitted in any form, by any means – electronic, mechanical, photocopying, recording, or otherwise – by anyone.

ISBN:

ISBN-13: 978-0-9785830-6-4

Published by Wake You Up Publishing 2025

Printed in the United States of America

This book is dedicated to all the members in The Fire Service – past, present, and future. May this book begin to build a culture that is inclusive and not exclusiv

Table of Contents

Foreword 1

    The Call to Purpose - Building the Why Behind the Will ... 1

CHAPTER ONE 5

Brick by Brick – Laying the Foundation 5

CHAPTER TWO 11

Motivation – The Factor 11

CHAPTER THREE 19

Determination - Persistence through the Flames 19

CHAPTER FOUR 23

Obstacles – Confronting Resistance with Resilience 23

CHAPTER FIVE 29

Goals – Defining Success and Reclaiming Purpose 29

CHAPTER SIX 37

Accountability – Owning the Work, Honoring the Weight 37

CHAPTER SEVEN 45

Organizational Culture – What You Normalize, You Authorize 45

CHAPTER EIGHT 53

Communication – The Bridge Between Isolation and Inclusion 53

CHAPTER NINE 63

Support Systems – The Strength of Unity 63

CHAPTER TEN 73

Stress Management – Finding Calm in the Storm 73

CHAPTER ELEVEN 83

Leadership in Crisis – Leading with Compassion 83

CHAPTER TWELVE 93

Preventing Burnout – Strategies for Sustainable Performance 93

CHAPTER THIRTEEN 105

The Power of Reflection – Learning from the Past 105

CHAPTER FOURTEEN 115

Navigating Change – Embracing Adaptability in the Fire Service 115

CHAPTER FIFTEEN **125**

Cultivating Emotional Intelligence – Enhancing Interpersonal Skills in the Fire Service **125**

CHAPTER SIXTEEN **135**

The Fire Service and Mental Health – Breaking the Stigma and Supporting Well-Being **135**

CHAPTER SEVENTEEN **145**

Building Resilience in Fire Service Personnel – The Power of Mental Toughness **145**

CHAPTER EIGHTEEN **155**

The Role of Leadership in Building a Resilient Fire Service Culture **155**

CHAPTER NINETEEN **165**

Leading with Empathy and Compassion **165**

CHAPTER TWENTY **175**

Building Trust Through Transparent Communication .. **175**

CHAPTER TWENTY-ONE **185**

Embracing Adaptability and Change **185**

CHAPTER TWENTY-TWO **195**

Supporting Mental Health and Well-Being in the Fire Service **195**

CHAPTER TWENTY-THREE **203**

Fostering a Positive Work Environment **203**

CHAPTER TWENTY-FIVE **223**

The Role of Leadership in Supporting Mental Health ... **223**

CHAPTER TWENTY-SIX **233**

Building Resilience in the Face of Crisis **233**

CHAPTER TWENTY-SEVEN **243**

The Importance of Psychological First Aid **243**

CHAPTER TWENTY-EIGHT **251**

The Need for Leadership and Support in Mental Health **251**

CHAPTER TWENTY-NINE **259**

Building Resilience in Firefighters **259**

CHAPTER THIRTY **267**

The Path Forward—Resilience and Mental Health as an Ongoing Journey **267**

CHAPTER THIRTY-ONE **277**

*EPILOGUE: The Legacy of Resilience and Leadership in
the Fire Service* 277

CHAPTER THIRTY-TWO 283

To DO 283

Foreword

The Call to Purpose - Building the Why Behind the Will

In every fire station, between the sound of tones dropping and boots hitting the ground, there's a quieter moment—one where each firefighter remembers why they chose this path. For some, it's the rush. For others, it's legacy or service. But no matter the reason, what unites us all is a call to purpose. A call not just to fight fire, but to endure, to grow, and to lead—even in the most chaotic and unkind environments.

This book began with a personal journey of motivation and goal-setting. At first glance, that journey might seem simple: identify a goal, face down obstacles, and achieve it. But as anyone in the fire service knows, the true path to success—especially when your world is burning, figuratively and literally—is rarely that clean. You don't just need goals; you need resilience. You don't just need motivation; you need meaning. And in today's fire service, what's too often missing is the leadership that makes those things sustainable.

Here's the hard truth: **poor leadership in the fire service is breaking people.** It's not just slowing promotions or muddying communication—it's compromising mental health, extinguishing passion, and leaving members isolated in a profession that's supposed to be about unity. Toxic cultures, unchecked egos, dismissive attitudes, and the failure to acknowledge the whole person behind the gear have created systems where burnout thrives and support is scarce.

But what if we could build differently?

Just like bricks stacked with care and intention, *resilience, compassion, and kinship* can be constructed into the very foundation of our leadership culture. Inspired by *The Wizard of Oz*, this book aims to reframe how we look at success, strength, and support in the fire service. Each chapter will explore how themes of motivation, determination, courage, and purpose intersect with the real-world challenges faced by fire personnel—especially when leadership fails.

Through personal stories, cultural analysis, and actionable tools, we will unpack how the size of your D.O.G. (Determination, Obstacles, Goals) can be measured not just by personal ambition, but by how well leadership supports—or sabotages—that ambition. We'll look at how the absence of emotionally intelligent leadership often forces members to choose between survival and authenticity, and how embracing resilience through kinship can rebuild what poor leadership tears down.

This isn't just a motivational journey—it's a fireground strategy for emotional survival.

So, before we move into tools, stories, and diagrams, ask yourself:

- Why did you answer the call in the first place?
- Has that call grown louder—or faded?
- And if leadership isn't helping you hear it clearly anymore, are you ready to build something better?

Brick by brick, you can reclaim your purpose. This is where the rebuilding begins.

What to Expect in the Chapters Ahead

This book is designed to be more than just a critical commentary on leadership failures in the fire service—it is a blueprint for transformation, resilience, and self-accountability. Built *brick by brick*, each chapter lays foundational insights that connect the harsh realities of professional burnout and emotional fatigue with the tools

needed to construct healthier leadership structures and more resilient individuals.

We journey down our own *Yellow Brick Road*—a metaphorical pathway through firehouse politics, emotional isolation, and professional despair—toward a deeper understanding of ourselves, our purpose, and our people. Along this path, we are guided by the framework of the D.O.G.: **Determination**, **Obstacles**, and **Goals**. Like Dorothy's journey through Oz, our road is lined with characters, conflicts, and revelations. Our "Toto" is *responsibility*—the persistent reminder of why we continue the mission, even when the storm rages.

Each chapter in this book introduces a *brick*—a principle or truth that helps build resilience in the face of chaos and cultivate kindness in the presence of kinship. These bricks are not ornamental; they are load-bearing. They support our mental health, our leadership credibility, and our organizational integrity.

This book doesn't just ask what's wrong—it shows how to make it right. Again, like Dorothy, we're not just trying to get back home; we're trying to discover who we really are along the way. Each chapter builds your inner and organizational resilience, brick by brick, so you can lead—first yourself, then others—through both chaos and conflict.

Enjoy!

CHAPTER ONE

Brick by Brick – Laying the Foundation

Chapter 1: Brick by Brick – Laying the Foundation

"Destiny is not a matter of chance; it is a matter of choice." – William Jennings Bryan

The Unseen Fire: Poor Leadership and Mental Health

In every firehouse, there are two types of fires. The ones we respond to — and the ones that burn quietly from within. We wear the badge. We face the flames. We stand in the chaos when others run from it. But this book is about a fire we don't often address — the one that can burn silently inside us. After over two decades in the fire service, I understand that firefighting isn't for the faint at heart. It's often thankless, underpaid, and requires immense sacrifice.

We all know the job. The alarm goes off, adrenaline spikes, and we answer the call — not just to fight fires, but to face trauma, tragedy, and the unknown. And then we're expected to go home, kiss our kids, mow the lawn, and act like everything is normal. But we know — it's not always normal. That chaos doesn't stay at the fireground. It can follow us home, haunt us in our sleep, fray our relationships, and eat away at our peace. That's why resilience isn't a luxury in this profession. It's survival.

And here's the truth: resilience is not built all at once or even in a day — It's built deliberately. Day by day. Call by call. Brick by brick.

Each brick is a choice:

- The choice to talk instead of bottle it up.
- The choice to ask for help instead of pretending you're fine.
- The choice to check in on your crew — not just physically, but mentally.
- The choice to breathe, to reflect, to rest.

In the chaos, we find strength. But in kindness, we build sustainability. Kindness — not just to others, but to yourself.

Thesis and Purpose

In the fire service, the toll of poor leadership isn't just organizational—it's deeply personal. Behind every burned-out firefighter, underperforming unit, or broken morale is often a chain of unaddressed leadership failures. This book, *B.R.I.C.K. by B.R.I.C.K.: (Building Resiliency in Chaos and Kindness by Being Resilient in Conflict and Kinship) …The Cost of Poor Leadership in the Fire Service*, examines how these failures contribute to serious mental health consequences for those on the front lines. Grounded in lived experience and supported by research on motivation, resilience, and organizational psychology, this text presents a resilience-based framework for addressing these challenges from the inside out.

At the center of this framework is a personal and professional philosophy I call the **D.O.G.—Determination, Obstacles, Goals**. It's a metaphorical tool and an introspective process: How big is your D.O.G.? How well are you equipped to persevere through hardship, confront systemic obstacles, and stay focused on your goals? And just as importantly, how is leadership helping—or hurting—that process?

This chapter sets the foundation for understanding how personal motivation, when misaligned with toxic leadership, becomes a catalyst for crisis. But it also offers hope: through self-assessment, structured goal-setting, and resilient thinking, individuals and organizations can reclaim their purpose and well-being—brick by brick.

The D.O.G. Philosophy: More Than a Metaphor

The concept of D.O.G. emerged from both personal

experience and countless conversations within the firehouse walls. Determination gives us forward momentum. Obstacles test our will. Goals give us direction. But what happens when the environment we operate in—specifically our leadership—works against that progression?

In *The Wizard of Oz*, Dorothy's journey home was filled with symbolic challenges. She was forced to navigate doubt (Scarecrow), detachment (Tin Man), and fear (Lion), all while being pushed forward by her sense of responsibility—embodied by her dog, Toto. In much the same way, firefighters face emotional, physical, and institutional obstacles daily, with their own "Totos"—bills, children, trauma, team dynamics—tugging at their conscience and fueling their drive.

Her journey was not just a quest for escape, but a process of transformation. The same can be said for those in our profession who navigate leadership voids and workplace dysfunction while trying to maintain personal integrity and motivation.

The Leadership-Mental Health Connection

Research by the National Fallen Firefighters Foundation, IAFF, and numerous mental health studies confirm that mental strain in the fire service is often *organizational*, not just operational. Poor communication, favoritism, inconsistent standards, and punitive environments erode trust and contribute to burnout, PTSD, and even suicide.

Leadership can be the strongest protective factor or the most corrosive risk factor for mental health in fire service personnel. The most resilient firefighter can still falter under toxic command.

When leaders fail to create psychologically safe, value-based workplaces, the results are profound:

- Resignation—mentally, if not physically
- Suppression of innovation
- Toxic competition
- Emotional exhaustion
- Increased incidents of anxiety, depression, and trauma responses

Why This Book, and Why Now?

This book is not a grievance. It is a call to transformation. Fire departments are undergoing scrutiny—from diversity and inclusion to budgetary transparency to mental health awareness. But one of the most overlooked elements of all is leadership accountability.

The next chapters will walk through a framework that blends:

- Motivational psychology (including Maslow's hierarchy)
- The D.O.G. model for internal navigation
- Real-world narratives from the fireground
- Organizational strategies for resilience and reform

Laying the First Brick

Resilience doesn't mean pretending nothing is wrong. It means confronting what *is* wrong while maintaining the will to build anyway. As we continue through this book, remember this: You don't have to fix the whole fire service. You just have to start with your brick—and lay it well.

CHAPTER TWO

Motivation – The Factor

Chapter 2: Motivation – The Factor

"Life takes on meaning when you become motivated, set goals and charge after them in an unstoppable manner."
— Les Brown

Motivation in the Fire Service

Motivation is the engine behind every meaningful action. In the fire service, where physical risk and emotional toll are constants, understanding what drives us becomes essential. But motivation doesn't occur in a vacuum. It is shaped by our environment, leadership, internal values, and, perhaps most powerfully, our responsibilities. If we are to address mental health issues in the fire service, we must begin with the honest assessment of what motivates those who serve.

This chapter explores how motivation functions not only as a personal driver but as a fragile element that leadership can either nurture or erode. When leadership fails to support, recognize, and inspire, the result is not just lower morale—it's psychological distress. This must change.

Motivation is the cornerstone of all progress.

In the fire service, we are often motivated by starting with a desire to serve, protect, and make a difference. However, this motivation is quickly tested by the realities of chaotic environments and leadership that lacks empathy or direction. To build resilience, we must begin by identifying our own Motivating Factors—those deep-rooted reasons that drive us, especially when circumstances are less than ideal.

Dorothy's journey in *The Wizard of Oz* parallels the path of a firefighter navigating their career. Her D.O.G.—Determination, Obstacles, and Goals—becomes a metaphor for the trials and motivations each of us faces. When leadership doesn't recognize our value or fails to provide guidance, we must return to our "Toto"—the responsibilities and personal values that first drove us to pursue this calling. Motivation under poor leadership isn't about blindly pressing forward; it's about purposefully setting goals despite resistance.

My journey into firefighting began with pure curiosity. While working at an immigration law firm in Herndon, Virginia, in 1997, our office overlooked the runways of Washington-Dulles Airport. From my third-floor window, I often watched the flashing lights of fire trucks responding to emergencies. Their presence was mesmerizing, and before long, I joined the Fairfax County Volunteer Fire Department.

Yes, we train hard to save lives. But mental health is not weakness — it's readiness. You cannot pour from an empty cup. You cannot rescue others if your own soul is drowning.

And so, we build:

- With peer support programs.
- With chaplains, counselors, and clinicians who get it.
- With a culture that stops saying "suck it up" and starts saying "I've got your back."

You don't have to carry every brick alone.

And sometimes, the bravest thing a firefighter can do isn't kicking down a door — it's sitting down and saying, "I'm not okay right now." This job will test you. The chaos will come. But together, brick by brick, we can build something stronger than fire: a culture of resilience rooted in brotherhood, in sisterhood, and in kindness.

Poor leadership is often the match that lights those internal fires.
Micromanagement, indifference, inconsistency, and ego-driven decisions — these don't just hurt morale. They fracture trust. They silence vulnerability. And worst of all,

they isolate us from one another.

When leadership fails to prioritize mental wellness, the weight of the job multiplies.
Stress turns into anxiety.
Fatigue becomes burnout. And trauma turns into long-term psychological wounds.

Let's be clear: firefighters are not immune to struggle.
We face death, devastation, and decisions that change lives in seconds.
What we need are leaders who understand that resilience isn't just toughness — it's **recovery**. It's **support**. It's **compassion with accountability**.

The D.O.G. Revisited: Fueling the Fire Within

The D.O.G. framework (Determination, Obstacles, Goals) reappears here as a way to frame our internal motivational state. Every firefighter has their own "Toto" — a responsibility, a purpose, a reason for entering the fire service in the first place. It might be family, service, duty, or financial stability. This driving force helps determine how resilient a person can be under pressure.

Consider the metaphor of Dorothy in *The Wizard of Oz*. Her motivation to protect her dog, Toto, led her on an unexpected journey filled with challenges. In the same way, our responsibilities push us into difficult environments, and it is motivation that allows us to persist through chaos. However, when leadership fails to validate or support that journey, motivation can become weaponized against the individual.

Maslow and Motivation: A Hierarchy of Needs

In 1954, psychologist Abraham Maslow introduced the Hierarchy of Needs, positing that humans are motivated by ascending levels of necessity:

1. **Physiological needs** (food, shelter, sleep)
2. **Safety needs** (security, order)
3. **Belongingness and love need** (relationships, team cohesion)
4. **Esteem needs** (recognition, respect)
5. **Self-actualization** (realizing personal potential)

In the fire service, failure of leadership often blocks progression at every level. Poor communication erodes safety. Toxic culture eliminates belonging. Lack of recognition crushes esteem. The cumulative effect is stagnation, burnout, or worse—mental health collapse.

Leaders who ignore these needs not only fail their teams; they inadvertently become obstacles. Instead of enabling growth, they force their personnel to fight for the basics.

The Cost of Disconnected Leadership

Motivation declines rapidly in environments where leadership is inconsistent, punitive, or indifferent. In my own experience, I entered the fire service energized and mission driven. Over time, repeated dismissals of ideas, lack of recognition, and a toxic evaluation process wore down that motivation. It wasn't that I lacked passion—it was that leadership repeatedly failed to fuel it.

Mental health research confirms this phenomenon. Studies show that employees with poor supervisors experience significantly higher rates of depression, anxiety, and emotional exhaustion. When leadership is seen as indifferent or hostile, personnel become disengaged, defensive, or despondent.

Reclaiming Motivation through Ownership

Motivation can be recovered through strategic self-advocacy. Creating a "self-promotion packet" that documents goals, tasks, and accomplishments helps restore ownership. It signals to both self and supervisors that your efforts matter, even if they go unrecognized.

This practice isn't about bragging; it's about survival. In high-risk, low-recognition environments, self-tracking becomes a psychological anchor. It fuels the internal narrative: *I am doing meaningful work. I am progressing.*

Protect Your Spark

Motivation is not indestructible. It requires nourishment, protection, and validation. Poor leadership can dim the brightest spark, but proactive strategies like documenting success, understanding your "why," and advocating for visibility can preserve it.

As we move into the next chapter on **Determination**, remember this: Motivation is the fire. Determination is the fuel. Without motivation, there is no reason to begin. Without determination, there is no way to continue.

So, what motivates you? And how are you protecting that spark in a system that sometimes forgets it exists?

CHAPTER THREE

Determination - Persistence through the Flames

Chapter 3: Determination - Persistence Through the Flames

Determination is the grit that keeps a firefighter advancing through smoke-filled hallways, the mental steel that allows a paramedic to maintain composure in chaos, and the internal flame that drives public servants to continue showing up despite overwhelming odds. In the fire service, determination is more than just a personal trait; it is a critical component of operational effectiveness and psychological endurance.

Yet determination does not grow in isolation. It is shaped and often strained by the culture and leadership environment in which firefighters operate. When leadership fails to support, recognize, or nourish the efforts of their personnel, determination can shift from a motivator to a martyrdom complex. Firefighters may keep pushing through adversity, but without institutional backing or mental health support, this persistence turns into silent suffering—a dangerous condition masked by stoicism.

In *Brick by Brick*, we explore resilience as a process of intentional building, not blind perseverance. Determination must be grounded in purpose, reinforced by kinship, and steered by sound leadership. Without these anchors, firefighters risk confusing stubbornness with strength. When leaders mistake burnout for dedication, they fail to intervene, thereby normalizing harmful work cultures and enabling systemic neglect.

Dorothy's journey in *The Wizard of Oz* metaphorically illustrates how persistence functions best when combined with insight and support. Her unwavering focus on returning home mirrors the fire service professional who pushes toward their goals despite hardship. But Dorothy was not alone—she had allies and a guiding purpose. In contrast, many firefighters operate in environments where leadership is absent or adversarial, leaving them to navigate personal and professional crises without support.

Poor leadership within the fire service often ignores the mental wear-and-tear that sustained determination demands. The cultural mantra of "just keep going" can eclipse the equally necessary directive of "know when to ask for help." Without clear examples from leadership that persistence includes seeking mental health support, many continue in silence, believing that struggle is proof of strength.

Academic studies have begun to underscore this concern. Research on first responder burnout and psychological distress reveals a direct correlation between poor supervisory relationships and higher rates of anxiety, depression, and occupational disengagement. Firefighters who feel unsupported or ignored by leadership are more likely to internalize failures, isolate themselves, or even leave the profession prematurely.

To realign the culture, leaders must model what healthy determination looks like. This includes acknowledging mental strain, celebrating incremental progress, and providing space for recovery. Command staff and supervisors set the tone—not just by their words but by how they treat setbacks and how they respond to vulnerability among their teams.

Fire service organizations must also implement structural supports: peer-support programs, mental health check-ins, and leadership development that teaches emotional intelligence alongside technical acumen. Resilience is not simply about pushing forward—it's about knowing when to pause, pivot, and protect your people.

Determination should be a shared ethic, not a solitary burden. When firefighters see their efforts recognized, their challenges validated, and their well-being prioritized, their persistence becomes sustainable. They stop surviving the job and start thriving in it.

In the next chapter, we will examine the "O" in D.O.G.—Obstacles—and how both internal and external barriers, especially those reinforced by poor leadership, can impede resilience, reduce motivation, and worsen mental health outcomes in the fire service.

CHAPTER FOUR

Obstacles – Confronting Resistance with Resilience

Chapter 4: Obstacles – Confronting Resistance with Resilience

The Fireground and the Frontline of Resistance

In both firefighting and life, obstacles are inevitable. Whether operational, emotional, or interpersonal, challenges arise that test our determination, professionalism, and resilience. In the fire service, however, many of these obstacles are not born from external hazards like heat, smoke, or collapsing structures, but from within— fueled by poor leadership, systemic neglect, and toxic workplace cultures.

When these internal barriers go unchecked, they foster organizational resistance that directly impacts mental health. The goal of this chapter is to examine how obstacles—particularly those created or intensified by dysfunctional leadership—can become chronic stressors, and how members of the fire service can develop resilience strategies to endure, adapt, and rise.

Defining Obstacles in the Fire Service Context

Obstacles in this field are rarely isolated incidents. They are layered, often institutional, and manifest as:

- **Micromanagement or absentee leadership** that undermines trust

- **Lack of emotional intelligence** in leadership during high-stress incidents

- **Unrealistic expectations** with minimal support

- **Discriminatory practices or cultural bias**

- **Resistance to innovation or feedback** from the line-level

These issues become barriers to not only performance but mental well-being, especially when firefighters feel unsupported or silenced.

The Psychological Toll of Organizational Resistance

When internal challenges mirror or exceed external dangers, they create what organizational psychologists call **"moral injury"**—the emotional trauma experienced when one's core values are violated by the systems or people trusted to uphold them. Firefighters experiencing this may report:

- Emotional fatigue and cynicism
- Withdrawal or feelings of helplessness
- Irritability, burnout, or increased substance use
- Symptoms of depression, anxiety, or PTSD

Research from the International Association of Fire Fighters (IAFF) and the National Fallen Firefighters Foundation (NFFF) consistently links poor internal support systems to increased mental health issues within departments.

Leadership as the Root of the Obstacle—or the Bridge Over It

Poor leadership acts as an accelerant to already stressful environments. For example:

- A captain who penalizes rather than mentors when mistakes are made
- Chiefs who reward loyalty over competency
- Supervisors who ignore bullying or toxic peer dynamics

Conversely, resilient and ethical leadership has been

shown to reduce these obstacles significantly. Leaders who model psychological safety, provide regular feedback, and engage in active listening can transform organizational resistance into a catalyst for team cohesion.

Building Resilience Against Internal Resistance

The metaphor from *The Wizard of Oz* becomes essential here: firefighters must construct their internal frameworks brick by brick—each brick representing a skill, habit, or support system that helps counterbalance the instability around them.

Strategies include:

- **Self-Assessment and Reflective Practice** – using journaling or counseling to process organizational stress

- **Boundary Setting** – understanding where personal responsibility ends and systemic dysfunction begins

- **Peer Resilience Networks** – small trusted groups that share experience and accountability

- **Training in Conflict Resolution** – learning to de-escalate internal tensions without undermining one's values

Case Study: When the Chain of Command Becomes a Chain of Constraint

Consider a firefighter named Marcus, who after five years of service was assigned a new lieutenant known for punitive discipline. Under this leader, Marcus's crew experienced micromanagement, public criticism, and a disregard for emotional well-being. Over time, absenteeism rose, morale plummeted, and Marcus began experiencing panic attacks before each shift.

The obstacle wasn't the job—it was the leadership style. Only when a new captain took over, bringing empathy and psychological safety to the crew, did things begin to change. Marcus was encouraged to seek counseling and became a peer support advocate.

His story exemplifies how poor leadership can transform typical challenges into enduring psychological obstacles, and how resilient leadership can restore purpose and pride.

Applying the D.O.G. Framework: Resistance Meets Insistence

In earlier chapters, we introduced the D.O.G. framework—Determination, Obstacles, and Goals. In the face of resistance, insistence becomes key. Insistence means maintaining focus and integrity even when surrounded by dysfunction. It is the active choice to keep building, advocating, and growing in the fire service, even when it feels like the system resists you.

Brick by Brick, Beyond the Resistance

Poor leadership and systemic resistance in the fire service can be disillusioning and damaging. But for those committed to the work—and to each other—resilience can be built one moment, one connection, one brick at a time. Whether you are a firefighter, officer, or administrator, it is your responsibility to either remove obstacles or help others build ladders over them.

The size of your D.O.G.—your persistence through resistance—determines the scale of what you can ultimately achieve.

CHAPTER FIVE

Goals – Defining Success and Reclaiming Purpose

Chapter 5: Goals – Defining Success and Reclaiming Purpose

Reconnecting to the "Why"

In the fire service, every mission begins with a clear objective—extinguish the fire, save the patient, preserve life. But ironically, many firefighters lose sight of their **personal goals** amid the constant crisis response and organizational noise. Over time, the "why" that once drove them into the career—service, pride, purpose—can fade behind bureaucracy, broken promises, and poor leadership.

This chapter unpacks how effective goal-setting serves as a protective factor against the mental health toll of a toxic work environment, and how leaders (or the lack thereof) either elevate or erode this critical component of professional resilience.

The Psychology of Goal-Setting in High-Stakes Environments

Goals give meaning to effort. In psychology, they serve not just as destination points, but as **anchors** that help us:

- Organize priorities

- Maintain a sense of progress

- Develop identity and personal agency

In trauma-heavy professions like firefighting, setting **intrinsic goals**—such as personal growth, competency, or mentorship—can buffer against burnout far more effectively than external ones like promotions or praise.

But in systems where poor leadership dominates, even the healthiest goals can become distorted. For example:

- Promotions may be awarded by favoritism rather than merit

- Innovation may be stifled by "we've always done it this way" mentalities

- Community impact may be overshadowed by internal politics

When this happens, the individual's internal compass is thrown off, and the result is often disengagement, frustration, or hopelessness.

When Goals Go Unacknowledged – A Mental Health Crisis in the Making

Firefighters are not exempt from the universal need for purpose. Studies show that **purposeful work is a critical driver of mental health**, and when goals are repeatedly invalidated or obstructed, individuals begin to experience:

- Chronic stress or burnout
- Decreased motivation or commitment
- Depression and anhedonia (loss of pleasure or interest)
- Heightened risk of suicide or substance misuse

This isn't due to a lack of ambition. It's often due to leadership that neither recognizes nor nurtures the developmental needs of its people.

The Organizational Role in Goal Frustration

Poor leadership in the fire service can derail goal-setting in several ways:

- **Lack of mentorship or coaching**: Young firefighters with potential are left unguided.

- **Hostile or dismissive supervisors**: Staff are discouraged from pursuing advancement or creative solutions.

- **Favoritism and inequity**: Promotions and opportunities are reserved for a select few, not based on qualification.

- **Punitive evaluation systems**: Employees focus more on avoiding reprimand than on pursuing meaningful goals.

These patterns foster a culture of stagnation and fear—both corrosive to mental health and mission success.

Reframing Goal-Setting Through the Resilience Lens

Drawing from *The Wizard of Oz*, we advocate a reframing of goals as **resilience markers**—conscious choices we make to keep building meaning despite dysfunction. This requires both strategic clarity and emotional courage. Resilient goal-setting involves:

- **Clarity**: Define not only what you want, but why you want it.

- **Autonomy**: Focus on goals within your control (skills, education, self-awareness).

- **Integration**: Align personal goals with team or community outcomes.

- **Documentation**: Keep a performance and development log—your "in-house résumé."

Just as Dorothy's journey in *The Wizard of Oz* was about more than reaching home—it was about transformation—so too must firefighters reframe goals as part of an ongoing personal evolution.

Case Study: Goal Misalignment and Burnout

Consider a firefighter named Elena. Early in her career, she set a goal to become a training officer. She studied rigorously, developed lesson plans, and mentored new recruits informally. However, her supervisor continually overlooked her contributions, favoring louder voices in the room. Over time, Elena's motivation waned. She began calling in sick more frequently, citing "exhaustion."

Eventually, a chief from another shift recognized her leadership potential and gave her a temporary training assignment. That validation reignited her drive. Today,

Elena serves as a senior instructor, and she frequently credits the turning point to that moment of goal **recognition**.

Her story reflects the profound impact leadership acknowledgment has on mental wellness—and the danger when it's absent.

Applying the D.O.G. Framework: Goal Pursuit as Purpose Recovery

In the D.O.G. model:

- **Determination** helps clarify what goals matter most
- **Obstacles** challenge those goals
- **Goals** themselves must be rooted in purpose, not politics

Your "G" isn't just a destination—it's a declaration: *I will not let poor leadership steal my sense of direction.* By setting meaningful goals, documenting your growth, and holding tight to your purpose, you preserve your identity and sanity in a system that may not always reward you.

Firefighters with Goals Become Architects of Resilience

You can't always change the environment, but you can change how you navigate it. Set goals that reflect your values. Track your progress, even if no one else sees it. Take ownership of your career, brick by brick. And remember: when leadership fails you, let your **goals remind you who you are**.

The size of your D.O.G.—your commitment to pursue your goals with purpose—shapes your fire service journey.

CHAPTER SIX

Accountability – Owning the Work, Honoring the Weight

Chapter 6: Accountability – Owning the Work, Honoring the Weight

The Responsibility We Carry

In the fire service, **accountability is non-negotiable**. Every call, every command, every action—or inaction—has real consequences. But while the front-facing operations often demand discipline and ownership, behind the scenes, many firefighters quietly battle organizational inconsistencies, unclear expectations, and hypocritical leadership.

When leaders fail to model accountability themselves, they create a double standard: firefighters are punished for mistakes, while supervisors deflect responsibility for systemic failures. This disconnect doesn't just harm performance—it **erodes morale**, **destroys trust**, and **fuels mental health crises**.

Redefining Accountability Beyond Punishment

Accountability is often mischaracterized as punishment. In reality, **true accountability is developmental**. It creates a culture where:

- Individuals take ownership of their actions
- Teams learn from mistakes without fear
- Leaders model the standards they expect

When accountability is rooted in retribution instead of growth, firefighters stop taking initiative. They hide errors instead of learning from them. They disengage, fearing every mistake will be weaponized.

Accountability should **empower**, not paralyze.

The Cost of Hypocritical Leadership

Poor leadership manifests in many subtle, toxic ways:

- Leaders who break rules they enforce on others
- Officers who fail to follow SOPs but micromanage subordinates
- Supervisors who never accept blame—but always assign it

This erodes psychological safety, creating environments where people protect themselves rather than protect each other. The mental toll includes:

- Increased anxiety and hypervigilance
- Emotional exhaustion
- Resentment and cynicism
- Quiet quitting or full disengagement

Leaders who demand accountability must first **model accountability**.

The Psychological Weight of High-Stakes Responsibility

Firefighters are trained to be accountable—to their teams, their tasks, and their communities. But when internal leadership lacks consistency, communication, or care, the weight becomes unsustainable. Over time, firefighters may experience:

- **Moral injury**: when personal ethics are compromised by organizational dysfunction
- **Survivor's guilt**: when poor decision-making from above leads to bad outcomes

- **Identity confusion**: "Am I a professional, or just a pawn?"

Without an affirming leadership structure, accountability turns into **self-blame**, leading to internalized stress, burnout, and shame.

Self-Accountability as a Tool of Resilience

In *Brick by Brick*, we affirm that ownership builds resilience—not perfection, but the willingness to reflect, admit, learn, and adjust.

Healthy self-accountability includes:

- **Self-monitoring**: tracking performance and progress
- **Self-advocacy**: voicing needs and setting boundaries
- **Documentation**: recording accomplishments, challenges, and solutions

These strategies protect mental health by reinforcing **autonomy** and **self-efficacy**, even when leadership structures fail to do so.

Systems of Accountability – Building from the Bottom Up

Poor leadership often stems from unclear or inconsistent accountability systems. Fire departments should formalize:

- Transparent evaluation criteria
- Peer review opportunities
- Leadership 360s (leaders evaluated by subordinates and peers)
- Check-ins on performance **and** wellbeing

When systems support **constructive accountability**, firefighters feel safer, more competent, and more engaged.

Case Study: The Unseen Labor of the High Performer

Marcus, a senior firefighter known for training new recruits, began noticing his extra efforts were not reflected in evaluations. His supervisor, overwhelmed and disengaged, rarely observed shifts. Eventually, Marcus was passed over for a promotion—given instead to a less-qualified but more politically connected colleague.

Marcus nearly left the department. But instead, he created

a **tracking log** for all extra tasks and initiatives, began copying his captain on performance emails, and documented outcomes. At the next evaluation cycle, the documentation forced recognition.

Marcus reclaimed power by **owning his work**, rather than waiting for flawed systems to notice it.

The D.O.G. Connection: Accountability Fuels Grit

- **Determination** keeps you focused even when you're overlooked.

- **Obstacles** test your ability to own your part without owning others' failures.

- **Goals** without accountability remain wishes. Ownership turns them into action.

Accountability isn't just about admitting when you're wrong. It's about being **visible** in your efforts, taking pride in your role, and building the integrity that poor leadership often tries to dismantle.

Brick by Brick, We Build Trust

Accountability—when practiced authentically—restores trust in the fire service. Trust between firefighter and officer.

Between firefighter and self. It protects mental health by removing the burden of shame and replacing it with ownership and dignity.

You may not control your evaluator, your chief, or the politics of your department. But you can control your **integrity**, your **documentation**, your **voice**, and your **worth**.

Hold the line—with accountability.

CHAPTER SEVEN

Organizational Culture – What You Normalize, You Authorize

Chapter 7: Organizational Culture – What You Normalize, You Authorize

The Culture We Breathe

In the fire service, culture isn't just a set of values on a wall. It's the air we breathe, the way we interact, and the stories we tell. It's the way new recruits are shaped, and how seasoned firefighters maintain their bearings. The culture of an organization either **supports or stifles resilience**, depending on how it is constructed and sustained.

When poor leadership fails to actively shape a culture of accountability, inclusivity, and emotional support, it normalizes dysfunction. It authorizes toxic behaviors that breed mental health struggles and disengagement. The key to resilience in the fire service lies in understanding the power of culture—and in actively shaping a culture that fosters well-being, teamwork, and mutual respect.

Defining Fire Service Culture

The culture within a fire department dictates **how things get done**, even when no one is watching. It encompasses:

- **Shared behaviors**: The day-to-day habits that people model for new recruits

- **Unwritten rules**: Norms that guide decisions in the absence of formal policies

- **Communication styles**: How conflict is handled and how information is shared

- **Emotional climate**: How emotions—especially stress—are expressed and managed

When the culture is healthy, people feel **supported**. When it is unhealthy, it creates environments where **toxic behaviors** like burnout, cynicism, and unresolved trauma thrive.

Toxic Culture: The Hidden Danger

Poor leadership often creates a **toxic culture** by tolerating behaviors that:

- Ignore or dismiss mental health needs

- Reward toxic machismo and discourage

vulnerability

- Encourage "toughing it out" rather than seeking help

- Normalize stress and trauma as part of the job

This normalization undermines the well-being of firefighters and compounds their mental health struggles. When these behaviors become ingrained, they lead to:

- **Emotional suppression**: Firefighters hide their struggles, fearing vulnerability will be punished or ridiculed.

- **Cynicism**: Over time, firefighters begin to distrust the department, feeling unsupported by leadership and fellow workers.

- **Burnout**: Chronic stress without adequate coping mechanisms leads to emotional and physical exhaustion.

By the time a firefighter reaches the point of mental collapse, the culture has already failed them.

Leadership's Role in Shaping Culture

Leaders are not only tasked with making decisions—they are responsible for shaping and maintaining the culture of the department. Their **actions speak louder than words**. When leaders consistently:

- Encourage open dialogue about mental health
- Model vulnerability and self-care
- Acknowledge the emotional toll of the job
- Enforce respectful communication and inclusivity

They create a culture where resilience can flourish. The fire service is inherently stressful, but **leaders who prioritize emotional well-being** normalize the message that resilience is not about ignoring hardship; it's about acknowledging it and seeking support when needed.

A Culture of Silence: The Silent Epidemic

In some fire departments, mental health is a **taboo topic**. Firefighters learn early that to survive in the fire service, they must put on a mask of toughness. They are expected to:

- **Ignore pain** and **push through adversity**
- **Hide vulnerabilities** and avoid showing any weakness
- **Compete** for the toughest job or toughest persona

This "silent epidemic" of emotional neglect keeps firefighters from seeking help, often until it's too late. If the culture remains silent about mental health, those struggling will suffer alone, and the effects will ripple through the entire organization, affecting morale, team cohesion, and overall performance.

Building a Resilient Culture: A Model for Change

It's possible to transform the culture of a fire department, but it requires conscious effort and intention. A **resilient culture** is one that:

- **Fosters psychological safety**: Firefighters feel comfortable talking about their struggles without fear of judgment or reprisal.

- **Celebrates vulnerability**: Recognizing that emotional strength is built by sharing, not hiding, difficulties.

- **Prioritizes wellness**: Departments encourage work-life balance, self-care, and mental health resources.

- **Leverages peer support**: A team that supports one another, particularly through tough situations, strengthens cohesion and promotes collective resilience.

In such a culture, **mental health is just as important as physical health**, and resilience is viewed as a team effort, not an individual burden.

Case Study: Changing the Tide

In a fire department that had long struggled with high turnover and widespread burnout, the new chief recognized that the culture needed transformation. The department had been known for its tough, stoic attitudes—firefighters were expected to deal with trauma alone, without ever showing weakness.

The new chief initiated several key changes:

- **Wellness checks**: Every firefighter had access to confidential mental health resources.

- **Open forums**: Regularly scheduled meetings where personnel could openly discuss challenges and successes, without fear of judgment.

- **Leadership training**: Officers were trained in emotional intelligence, active listening, and fostering a supportive environment for their teams.

The results were noticeable within months:

- Turnover decreased
- Team morale improved
- Firefighters began seeking help when needed
- Performance and trust levels rose significantly

The culture shifted from **"tough it out"** to **"together, we rise"**.

The D.O.G. Connection: Cultivating a Resilient Culture

A resilient culture fosters an environment where **ownership** of mental health and well-being becomes collective:

- **Determination** drives the commitment to creating a culture of care.
- **Obstacles** are tackled through support, collaboration, and shared responsibility.
- **Goals** for mental health, teamwork, and personal growth are celebrated.

A fire department that embraces this shift from a toxic to a resilient culture sets the stage for a **stronger, healthier**

workforce, one that can better handle the chaos and kindness that come with the job.

Shaping Culture, Shaping Resilience

In the fire service, culture is a living organism. It evolves with the actions of its members, shaped by leaders who prioritize people over performance. A **toxic culture** leaves no room for mental health, resilience, or recovery. But a **resilient culture** supports every firefighter in their journey to heal, grow, and thrive.

As we normalize supportive behaviors and empathetic leadership, we begin to author a culture where resilience isn't an exception—it's the expectation.

CHAPTER EIGHT

Communication – The Bridge Between Isolation and Inclusion

Chapter 8: Communication – The Bridge Between Isolation and Inclusion

The Lifeblood of Connection

Communication is the pulse of any organization. In the fire service, it's not just about dispatch calls or tactical instructions—it's about how we **connect, share, and build relationships** within the team. Poor communication can lead to confusion, isolation, and broken trust. But effective communication—open, honest, and supportive—builds **stronger relationships, fosters mental well-being,** and enhances **resilience**.

In the fire service, where high-stress environments and life-or-death decisions are common, **communication can be the bridge between isolation and inclusion**. When leaders fail to establish clear, transparent, and empathetic communication, it creates gaps that lead to **emotional and psychological detachment**, impacting both individual and team resilience.

Communication Breakdown: The Impact of Silence

In many fire departments, communication often becomes **transactional**—a back-and-forth of instructions and operational needs. However, the **lack of emotional communication** is where many departments fail. When leaders and team members do not engage in **meaningful conversations** about mental health, challenges, or personal well-being, it leads to **isolation**.

This lack of open communication creates:

- **Emotional disconnection**: Firefighters feel like their struggles are unimportant or unspoken.

- **Unaddressed mental health issues**: Without communication about mental health, firefighters may not know how or when to seek help, or they might feel ashamed for doing so.

- **Cynicism and disengagement**: If issues are never discussed, a sense of detachment can set in. Firefighters may begin to feel like they are alone in their struggles, causing morale to plummet.

The negative effects are compounded when leaders fail to recognize their role in encouraging open dialogue. In the absence of positive, intentional communication, silence becomes the default—one that fosters mental health challenges such as burnout, anxiety, and depression.

The Power of Transparent Communication

Transparent communication is **the antidote to isolation**. Leaders in the fire service must go beyond functional or task-based communication to create an environment where **feelings, struggles, and victories are shared openly**. When leaders model vulnerability and openness, they encourage others to do the same.

Key aspects of transparent communication include:

- **Active listening**: Leaders should not just speak to their teams—they need to listen. Active listening ensures that firefighters feel heard and valued, which builds trust and emotional safety.

- **Clear expectations**: Communication must be clear regarding job expectations and mental health resources available. Misunderstandings often breed frustration and disengagement.

- **Providing feedback**: Feedback is essential for growth, but it must be constructive and supportive. Positive feedback enhances confidence, while negative feedback, when communicated properly, can lead to improvement without damaging morale.

When transparent communication becomes a **core value**, it eliminates the barriers to connection, ensuring that every firefighter feels valued, heard, and understood. This creates an environment where **resilience** is not just supported but actively encouraged.

Empathy in Leadership: The Human Element

A key element in communication is **empathy**—understanding and sharing the feelings of others. In fire service leadership, empathy is often overlooked in favor of decisiveness or toughness. However, **empathy is critical** to the resilience of both individuals and teams.

Leaders who lead with empathy:

- **Acknowledge the emotional toll of the job**: They don't downplay the stress and trauma that come with firefighting but recognize them as real challenges.

- **Foster emotional support**: Leaders should actively encourage their teams to seek support from each other and from mental health professionals when needed.

- **Model emotional intelligence**: Empathy requires leaders to regulate their own emotions and be aware of the emotional dynamics of their team. Emotional intelligence enables leaders to navigate difficult conversations and manage high-stress situations with compassion.

By emphasizing empathy in communication, leaders can create an environment where team members feel understood and supported. This emotional connection is essential for **mental well-being** and enables firefighters to **build resilience together**, knowing that they can rely on one another during the toughest of times.

Creating a Culture of Inclusivity Through Communication

Inclusivity in communication means ensuring that every firefighter feels they have a voice. Poor leadership often results in a **hierarchical communication structure** that limits open dialogue, especially between ranks. When communication flows in only one direction—from the top down—firefighters can feel isolated, disempowered, and unsupported.

A culture of inclusivity through communication looks like:

- **Encouraging feedback from all levels**: Leaders should actively seek input from firefighters at every rank and role, ensuring that everyone's perspective is heard and valued.

- **Promoting team collaboration**: Encouraging teamwork in discussions, decision-making, and problem-solving leads to stronger relationships and better outcomes.

- **Celebrating diversity**: Inclusivity goes beyond role and rank—it means embracing different perspectives, experiences, and backgrounds. When leaders embrace and celebrate diversity in communication, they create a team that is more adaptable and unified.

In an inclusive environment, team members are more likely to reach out for help, share their experiences, and support one another. **Inclusivity fosters resilience**, ensuring that everyone feels part of the collective effort, no matter the challenges.

Communication Strategies for Mental Health Awareness

Fire departments need to adopt communication strategies that **actively promote mental health awareness**. The stigma surrounding mental health often keeps firefighters from seeking the help they need. However, by integrating mental health discussions into everyday communication, this stigma can be reduced or eliminated.

Effective strategies include:

- **Normalizing mental health conversations**: Leaders should talk openly about their own mental health challenges and encourage others to do the same.

- **Providing resources and information**: Communicating the availability of mental health resources, peer support groups, and counseling services should be part of everyday dialogue, not an afterthought.

- **Creating safe spaces for discussion**: Providing private settings for team members to discuss personal challenges without fear of judgment can significantly reduce the stigma surrounding mental health.

When mental health becomes a normalized topic in fire service communication, it allows firefighters to feel more comfortable seeking help. **Resilience** is strengthened because team members know that emotional support is accessible and encouraged.

Case Study: The Power of Open Communication in Action

A fire department struggling with high stress, burnout, and disengagement made a commitment to improve communication. The chief initiated regular **team huddles**, where every firefighter had the opportunity to speak up about their challenges, both personal and professional. They implemented **mental health check-ins**, allowing everyone to discuss their emotional well-being openly.

The results were transformative:

- **Employee engagement** skyrocketed as firefighters felt more connected to their colleagues.

- **Burnout rates decreased** because the culture of communication created a supportive environment where stress could be addressed.

- **Team cohesion** improved, as members knew they could rely on each other for both operational and emotional support.

This case study shows that with **intentional communication**, fire departments can create an environment where mental health is prioritized, resilience is cultivated, and team members are empowered.

Communication and the D.O.G. Framework: Cultivating Resilience Together

The **D.O.G. Framework** applies to communication in powerful ways:

- **Determination**: Effective communication helps everyone understand their roles and responsibilities, keeping the team focused on shared goals.

- **Obstacles**: When communication is clear and empathetic, obstacles—whether emotional or operational—are easier to overcome as a team.

- **Goals**: Communicating about individual and team goals ensures that everyone is on the same page and working toward a common purpose.

When communication is open, inclusive, and empathetic, resilience is built from the ground up, with every firefighter contributing to the culture of care and support.

Communication as the Backbone of Resilience

The importance of communication in fostering resilience in the fire service cannot be overstated. It is the **bridge between isolation and inclusion**, the tool that connects individuals to each other and to the mission. By prioritizing transparent, empathetic, and inclusive communication, fire departments can **build a culture of resilience** that supports every firefighter in the face of adversity.

As leaders, firefighters, and colleagues, we must remember that the words we speak, the actions we take, and the support we offer are what make **resilience** not just an individual goal, but a **collective strength**. Communication is the key to unlocking that strength—let's ensure it is a strength we continue to develop.

CHAPTER NINE

Support Systems – The Strength of Unity

Chapter 9: Support Systems – The Strength of Unity

The Power of Collective Strength

In a high-pressure, high-stakes profession like firefighting, support systems are not just important—they are essential. **Resilience** in the fire service is not an individual achievement; it is a collective effort. When firefighters face the challenges of trauma, stress, and burnout, it is the support of their team and community that helps them stand strong. **Unity** in the fire service is the foundation of resilience, and the systems that support it are what allow individuals to thrive even in the face of adversity.

In this chapter, we will explore how **support systems**—from the team to external resources—serve as the backbone for **mental health, resilience**, and **motivation** in the fire service. We will discuss the critical importance of **peer support, mentorship**, and **organizational culture** in fostering mental well-being and building **resilient teams**.

The Role of Peer Support: Strength in Numbers

The nature of firefighting is inherently isolating—often, the physical and emotional weight of the job can lead to feelings of **loneliness** and **disconnection**. One of the most powerful tools for combating these feelings is **peer support**. Peer support programs within fire departments allow firefighters to lean on one another, sharing experiences, challenges, and strategies for coping.

Peer support is invaluable for several reasons:

- **Shared experience**: Peer supporters understand the specific challenges and stresses of firefighting, providing a safe space for vulnerable conversations.

- **Anonymity and trust**: Peer support often feels less formal than professional counseling, which can encourage more firefighters to seek help without fear of judgment.

- **Faster response**: Peer support networks allow for immediate, in-the-moment support when needed most—whether on the fireground or after a traumatic incident.

Peer support programs are vital because they create **mutual understanding** and provide **emotional validation** that reduces feelings of isolation. Firefighters who know they are supported by their peers are more likely to engage in healthy coping strategies and seek additional help if needed.

Mentorship: Building Resilience Through Experience

Mentorship is another cornerstone of support systems in the fire service. An effective mentor not only teaches technical skills but also guides **emotional resilience**. Firefighters at all levels benefit from the wisdom of those with more experience, who can share insights on how to cope with the emotional toll of the job and how to approach difficult situations with mental clarity.

Mentorship can have several significant benefits:

- **Knowledge transfer**: Experienced mentors pass on critical knowledge about both the technical and emotional aspects of the job.

- **Personal growth**: A strong mentor-mentee relationship provides emotional guidance, helping the mentee to manage stress, trauma, and burnout.

- **Building confidence**: By having a trusted mentor, mentees are more likely to feel empowered to take on leadership roles themselves, thereby contributing to the overall resilience of the department.

In many cases, mentors can also identify early warning signs of mental health issues, offering support before problems escalate. These relationships are **protective factors** against the isolation and mental health struggles that often arise in firefighting.

The Importance of Organizational Culture in Building Support Systems

While peer support and mentorship are powerful, they must be supported by a broader **organizational culture** that prioritizes mental health and resilience. **Culture** defines how support systems are structured and how they operate within the fire service. When leaders foster a culture of care, collaboration, and open dialogue, they make it easier for support systems to flourish.

A supportive organizational culture:

- **Reduces stigma**: When leaders openly talk about mental health, it signals to the team that it is okay to seek help. This can reduce the shame and stigma associated with mental health issues, making it more likely that firefighters will reach out when they need support.

- **Fosters community**: A positive culture helps build stronger connections between team members, increasing feelings of belonging and reducing isolation.

- **Promotes balance**: Organizational cultures that support work-life balance and recognize the importance of downtime reduce burnout and stress levels among employees.

Creating a culture that celebrates **mental well-being** allows firefighters to build resilience together. When the organizational environment supports mental health, it provides a **foundation of stability**, which in turn strengthens the team's ability to face any challenge.

External Resources: Expanding the Support Network

While peer support, mentorship, and a strong organizational culture are essential, **external resources** play a key role in comprehensive support systems. External mental health professionals, community groups, and wellness programs provide additional layers of support that are crucial when internal resources are not enough.

External resources might include:

- **Therapists and counselors**: Firefighters who need professional mental health support can rely on qualified counselors who understand the unique challenges of the profession.

- **Employee Assistance Programs (EAPs)**: EAPs provide confidential counseling, crisis management, and other resources to employees and their families.

- **Support groups**: Peer-led support groups for mental health issues, trauma, and stress can offer ongoing emotional support in a group setting.

- **Physical wellness programs**: Physical fitness and wellness programs that promote overall well-being can help reduce the mental strain of the job.

By encouraging firefighters to access external support resources, departments can help them develop **holistic resilience**, taking care of their **mental, emotional, and physical health**. Fire departments that integrate external resources into their support systems show their commitment to **long-term well-being**.

Building a Unified Support System: Collaboration Is Key

To be most effective, support systems must be **collaborative**. Peer support, mentorship, organizational culture, and external resources all play different but complementary roles in the broader support network. When these systems are interconnected, firefighters are more likely to feel supported at every level—from their teammates on the front lines to their supervisors and external professionals.

A unified support system has several key features:

- **Clear communication**: Support systems must be well-communicated so that every firefighter knows what resources are available and how to access them.

- **Ongoing training**: Regular training on mental health awareness, peer support techniques, and how to access external resources helps ensure that everyone knows how to navigate the system.

- **Feedback and improvement**: Support systems should evolve based on feedback from the team. Leaders should regularly assess the effectiveness of existing support systems and make adjustments as needed.

A collaborative approach ensures that no firefighter ever feels like they are alone in their struggles, and that they have access to the appropriate help at every stage of their career.

Case Study: Strengthening Support Systems in a Fire Department

A fire department located in a high-stress urban area struggled with high turnover, burnout, and a lack of morale. After a department-wide survey revealed that many firefighters felt isolated and unsupported, the leadership team decided to prioritize **building a more robust support system**.

The changes they implemented included:

- **Peer support groups**: These were established to provide immediate, confidential emotional support for those who had experienced trauma.

- **Mentorship programs**: Senior firefighters began mentoring newer recruits, offering guidance both on the job and in managing stress.

- **Mental health resources**: The department partnered with an EAP and encouraged firefighters to use counseling services when needed.

- **Physical wellness programs**: A new fitness regimen was introduced, focusing on stress relief and overall health.

Over the course of a year, the department saw **a significant decrease in turnover rates, higher levels of job satisfaction**, and **lower rates of burnout**. Firefighters reported feeling more connected to their peers and better equipped to manage the stress of the job.

This case study shows that **investing in support systems** not only improves mental health outcomes but also strengthens the department as a whole, creating a more resilient and cohesive team.

The D.O.G. Framework and Support Systems: Collective Resilience

The **D.O.G. Framework—Determination, Obstacles, and Goals**—can also be applied to support systems in the fire service:

- **Determination**: A strong support system instills a sense of determination in each firefighter, knowing they are not alone in facing obstacles.

- **Obstacles**: Support systems help firefighters navigate the inevitable obstacles they face, from traumatic incidents to personal challenges, without feeling defeated.

- **Goals**: The support network helps firefighters set and achieve personal and professional goals, from improving mental well-being to advancing in their careers.

When firefighters have a **support system** that helps them stay determined, overcome obstacles, and achieve their goals, they are better equipped to thrive under pressure. This unified strength is essential to building **resilience** in the fire service.

The Collective Strength of Support Systems

Support systems are essential to the mental health and resilience of firefighters. They provide the emotional, psychological, and physical support needed to navigate the challenges of the job. By prioritizing **peer support**, **mentorship**, and a **strong organizational culture**, fire departments can create environments where firefighters feel supported, heard, and empowered.

When external resources are integrated into the support system, it ensures that every firefighter has access to the help they need. Building a **unified, collaborative support network** strengthens the entire team and enables firefighters to build resilience together, facing challenges not as individuals, but as a unified force.

CHAPTER TEN

Stress Management – Finding Calm in the Storm

Chapter 10: Stress Management – Finding Calm in the Storm

The Pressure of Firefighting

Firefighting is a profession that inherently involves **stress**, both physical and emotional. Whether it's the pressure of saving lives, the physical demands of the job, or the mental toll of witnessing trauma, stress is a constant companion for firefighters. Yet, how firefighters manage this stress can significantly impact their **resilience**, **mental health**, and overall effectiveness on the job.

This chapter explores how firefighters can manage stress effectively, **prevent burnout**, and maintain their mental well-being through **stress management** techniques. We will discuss **strategies**, **tools**, and **mindset shifts** that help firefighters navigate the intense pressures of their work, ultimately fostering greater **resilience** both individually and collectively.

Understanding Stress: The Silent Challenge

Stress is a normal reaction to the demands and challenges of life. However, when left unaddressed, **chronic stress** can have serious physical and emotional consequences. In firefighting, stress often comes in the form of **critical incidents**, long shifts, high-stakes situations, and exposure to trauma. The unpredictable nature of the job makes it difficult to anticipate when or how stress will strike.

There are two types of stress:

- **Acute stress**: This is the immediate stress response to a specific situation. It's often experienced during emergencies when a firefighter must react quickly and decisively.

- **Chronic stress**: This is the prolonged, ongoing stress that accumulates over time. Chronic stress can result from **long hours**, **trauma exposure**, or **workplace tension**.

Understanding stress and its effects is the first step in managing it. **Acute stress** can be harnessed to **fuel performance** during emergencies, while **chronic stress** requires long-term strategies to mitigate its effects.

The Impact of Stress on Firefighters' Mental Health

The effects of chronic stress can be far-reaching, especially for those in high-pressure jobs like firefighting. The combination of physical, emotional, and psychological stressors can lead to significant **mental health challenges**, including:

- **Burnout**: Emotional exhaustion, detachment, and reduced performance due to prolonged exposure to stress.

- **PTSD**: Post-traumatic stress disorder resulting from exposure to traumatic events, such as witnessing death or severe injury.

- **Anxiety and depression**: Feelings of hopelessness, constant worry, and sadness stemming from prolonged stress.

- **Substance abuse**: Some firefighters may turn to alcohol or drugs as a way to cope with stress and emotional pain.

When stress is not managed effectively, these mental health challenges can compound, leading to **decreased job performance, increased absenteeism**, and a **higher rate of attrition** in fire departments.

It's important to recognize the signs of stress early and to have strategies in place to manage it before it escalates into something more severe.

Stress Management Strategies for Firefighters

Managing stress is not about eliminating it, but about learning to cope with it in healthy ways. The goal is not to avoid stress but to **build resilience** in the face of it. Below are several **evidence-based stress management techniques** that can help firefighters navigate the challenges of their profession.

Mindfulness and Meditation

Mindfulness is the practice of being present in the moment, without judgment. It has been shown to reduce stress, improve focus, and increase emotional regulation. For firefighters, mindfulness can be a critical tool for managing stress during high-pressure situations.

- **Breathing exercises**: Slow, deep breathing helps activate the **parasympathetic nervous system**, reducing heart rate and promoting calmness.

- **Meditation**: Regular meditation practice can help firefighters create space between the stimuli they experience and their reactions, reducing the emotional impact of stress.

- **Mindful awareness**: Being present and aware of one's thoughts, feelings, and physical sensations can help firefighters stay grounded during stressful situations.

Mindfulness and meditation are effective for both acute stress in the field and chronic stress after a tough shift or incident.

Physical Exercise

Exercise is one of the most effective ways to reduce stress. Physical activity boosts the release of **endorphins**, the body's natural mood elevators, and improves sleep quality. For firefighters, regular exercise helps maintain physical fitness and stamina, which are essential for the job, while also providing an outlet for stress relief.

- **Strength training**: Builds muscle and enhances physical endurance, helping firefighters manage the physical demands of the job.

- **Cardio exercises**: Running, swimming, or cycling can reduce anxiety and improve cardiovascular health.

- **Stretching**: Yoga or simple stretching exercises can

reduce tension and improve flexibility.

Physical fitness and stress management are deeply intertwined; staying physically fit enables firefighters to handle the mental and emotional strain of the job with more resilience.

Sleep Hygiene

Stress and sleep are tightly linked. When firefighters experience **chronic stress**, their sleep patterns are often disrupted, leading to further stress and emotional burnout. Improving **sleep hygiene**—the habits and practices that contribute to good quality sleep—is crucial for managing stress.

- **Establish a routine**: Going to bed and waking up at the same time each day helps regulate the body's internal clock.

- **Create a restful environment**: Minimizing noise, light, and distractions can create an environment conducive to deep sleep.

- **Limit caffeine and alcohol**: Both can disrupt sleep, especially when consumed in the evening.

Getting enough restful sleep improves focus, reduces irritability, and increases overall resilience to stress.

Social Support and Connection

One of the greatest antidotes to stress is connection. Building strong relationships with peers, family, and friends provides a supportive foundation for dealing with stress. Having someone to talk to, share experiences with, or simply laugh with can reduce the impact of stress.

- **Peer support groups**: As discussed in Chapter 9, connecting with others who understand the unique stresses of firefighting provides comfort and camaraderie.

- **Family support**: Family members can offer emotional support and serve as a source of stability during times of stress.

- **Therapeutic relationships**: Speaking with a counselor or therapist allows for emotional release and healing from trauma.

Strong social support networks provide a **buffer** against stress, enabling firefighters to **navigate challenges more effectively**.

Time Management and Relaxation

Firefighters often face long shifts, irregular hours, and a heavy workload. Effective **time management** ensures that there is time to decompress, relax, and rejuvenate between shifts.

- **Prioritize tasks**: Focus on the most important and urgent tasks first to reduce feelings of overwhelm.

- **Take breaks**: Regular breaks during a shift help manage physical and mental fatigue.

- **Hobbies and interests**: Engage in activities outside of work that bring joy and relaxation, such as reading, gardening, or spending time with loved ones.

Time management techniques reduce stress by helping firefighters balance their personal and professional responsibilities, ensuring that they have time for rest and recovery.

Creating a Stress-Resilient Department Culture

While individual strategies are essential for stress management, departments must also foster a culture that prioritizes **stress resilience**. Leaders play a critical role in promoting stress management and creating an environment where **mental well-being** is as important as physical fitness.

- **Encourage open discussions**: Leaders should normalize conversations about stress and mental health within the department.

- **Offer resources**: Departments should provide access to stress management tools, such as wellness programs, mental health services, and training on stress reduction techniques.

- **Model healthy behaviors**: Leaders who demonstrate stress management techniques and prioritize self-care set an example for the rest of the team.

By creating a **culture of stress resilience**, fire departments can reduce the impact of stress on individual firefighters and improve overall team performance.

Case Study: A Fire Department's Stress Management Initiative

A fire department in a busy urban area faced high levels of burnout and stress-related attrition. In response, the leadership team implemented a **department-wide stress management initiative** that included mindfulness training, physical fitness programs, sleep education, and social support activities.

The results were clear:

- **Reduced burnout**: Firefighters reported feeling less

emotionally drained and more connected to their peers.

- **Increased retention**: Firefighters were more likely to stay in the department due to improved job satisfaction and mental well-being.

- **Improved performance**: Firefighters showed higher levels of energy and focus on the job, leading to better performance on emergency scenes.

The success of this initiative highlights the importance of **department-wide support systems** for stress management and the impact of a holistic approach to mental health.

Building Resilience Through Stress Management

Stress is an unavoidable aspect of firefighting, but it doesn't have to be debilitating. By employing **effective stress management techniques**, firefighters can learn to **navigate stress** with greater resilience, ensuring that it doesn't take a toll on their mental health or performance.

As individuals and as a collective, firefighters must prioritize stress management to stay resilient in the face of the **demands** of the job. With the right tools, support, and mindset, they can remain **strong** and capable, even in the face of the storm.

CHAPTER ELEVEN

Leadership in Crisis – Leading with Compassion

Chapter 11: Leadership in Crisis – Leading with Compassion

The Heart of Leadership

In any high-stakes environment, especially within the fire service, leadership is paramount to **success**. During a crisis, a leader's ability to remain calm, composed, and compassionate can mean the difference between **chaos** and **order**, between **failure** and **success**. For firefighters, a leader who leads with compassion not only drives the team's effectiveness but also promotes **mental health, resilience,** and **safety**.

This chapter delves into the role of leadership in **high-pressure situations**, particularly in moments of crisis. We explore the importance of **compassionate leadership**, how it can transform the experience of both the individual firefighter and the team, and how it fosters a culture of **empathy, trust**, and **mental well-being**.

The Essence of Compassionate Leadership

Compassionate leadership is defined by the ability to lead with **empathy** and **understanding**, especially in moments of crisis. In the context of firefighting, this involves not just guiding your team through a critical incident but doing so with a deep recognition of the emotional and mental strain that your team members may be experiencing.

A compassionate leader actively listens, is approachable, and creates an environment where people feel **safe** to share their **fears, concerns,** and **emotions**. They lead with a clear understanding that stress, trauma, and mental health challenges are real and impactful, and they support their team members in addressing these challenges.

Effective leadership in crisis, especially when **emotions run high**, is built on the following key components:

- **Empathy**: Understanding the feelings and experiences of others.

- **Active Listening**: Offering full attention and validation to the concerns of others.

- **Supportive Actions**: Taking steps to alleviate stress, provide resources, or guide individuals through tough situations.

-

This compassionate approach does not weaken a leader; rather, it builds trust and cultivates an environment where firefighters feel **valued, understood,** and **supported.**

Leading with Compassion During a Crisis

During a crisis, the need for quick decision-making, **clear communication**, and decisive action is essential. However, equally important is the role of a leader who provides a **sense of calm**, assures their team that they are **not alone**, and demonstrates **emotional intelligence** in their actions. Compassionate leadership can significantly impact how firefighters react to high-stress situations, both during the crisis itself and in the aftermath.

Calm Under Pressure

A compassionate leader remains **composed** in the face of uncertainty. This calmness is **contagious**, and when a leader can stay focused and present, their team is more likely to mirror that behavior. Compassionate leadership ensures that decisions are made with clarity and **thoughtfulness**, not out of panic or haste.

When a leader responds with calmness, it helps firefighters navigate difficult situations with a **clear mind**, reducing emotional overload and increasing the likelihood of effective decision-making.

Emotional Support During Trauma

Firefighters are often exposed to traumatic events, and the emotional toll can be heavy. A compassionate leader recognizes the **psychological effects** of trauma and provides emotional support. This support can come in the form of:

- **Debriefings**: After a particularly difficult call or event, debriefings help firefighters process their emotions, talk through what happened, and provide peer support.

- **Check-ins**: Leaders should actively check in on their team, asking how they're feeling and if they need additional support.

- **Access to Resources**: Ensuring that firefighters have access to mental health resources, such as counseling, peer support programs, or stress management workshops.

By offering these resources, a compassionate leader not only supports the mental well-being of their team but also promotes a **culture of care** within the department.

Promoting Mental Health Awareness

Compassionate leaders are advocates for **mental health awareness** and work to reduce the stigma around seeking help. By normalizing conversations about **mental health**, leaders encourage firefighters to prioritize their well-being. This proactive approach to mental health ensures that firefighters feel empowered to **ask for help** when needed, leading to better long-term outcomes.

Leaders who openly discuss mental health create a culture where firefighters are more likely to seek support before stress or trauma leads to more severe issues, such as **burnout, depression,** or **PTSD**.

Compassionate Leadership and Its Impact on Firefighter Well-Being

The impact of compassionate leadership extends beyond **crisis moments**. A leader who consistently demonstrates empathy, understanding, and emotional support builds an environment where mental health is prioritized, and resilience is nurtured.

Building Trust and Loyalty

When firefighters feel supported by their leaders, they are more likely to trust them. Trust, in turn, fosters loyalty and cooperation within the team. Compassionate leadership creates a **safe environment** where team members feel they can **speak openly** without fear of judgment, leading to improved communication and collaboration.

In a crisis, this trust is invaluable. When firefighters know they are supported by their leader, they are more likely to stay focused and make sound decisions, even under pressure.

Reducing Burnout and Attrition

High levels of stress and exposure to trauma can lead to **burnout**—a state of emotional exhaustion that can severely impact performance and overall well-being. Compassionate leadership plays a significant role in reducing burnout by:

- Providing **regular support** and recognition for hard work.

- Encouraging **work-life balance** and time off to recharge.

- Addressing **emotional needs** before they turn into burnout or depression.

When firefighters feel supported by their leaders, they are less likely to experience burnout and more likely to remain in the profession long-term, maintaining **higher levels of job satisfaction** and **mental health.**

Creating a Resilient Team

A compassionate leader doesn't just manage the well-being of individuals—they work to build a **resilient team**. Resilient teams are able to **adapt** to stress, recover from challenges, and support one another during difficult times. Compassionate leadership fosters an environment where mutual **trust**, **empathy**, and **collaboration** are the norm.

By emphasizing team unity and emotional support, compassionate leadership creates a workforce that is equipped to handle the mental and emotional challenges of the fire service while maintaining **high performance** under stress.

Leading by Example: Modeling Compassionate Leadership

Effective leaders don't just tell their team members how to behave—they model the behaviors they wish to see. By consistently demonstrating compassion, emotional intelligence, and support, leaders set the tone for the entire department.

Leaders who make their own well-being a priority and who seek **support** when needed show their team that it's **okay to not be okay** and that **mental health matters**. By leading with compassion, leaders not only inspire their team but also create a **culture of care** that can withstand even the most difficult challenges.

Case Study: Compassionate Leadership in Action

In a rural fire department, the Chief implemented a leadership strategy focused on compassionate support during a particularly high-stress period. The department had recently experienced a series of traumatic incidents, and morale was low. The Chief introduced weekly check-ins with all firefighters, as well as a mental health support program.

As a result:

- Firefighters reported **feeling more supported** and less isolated.

- Burnout rates decreased significantly.

- The department experienced **improved performance** and a higher sense of **team cohesion**.

The compassionate approach allowed the team to process the stress of their work more effectively, fostering both mental health and resilience in the long term.

Compassionate Leadership – The Heartbeat of Resilience

Compassionate leadership is not a **soft skill**—it is a **crucial** element of building a **resilient, high-performing fire department**. Leaders who lead with compassion inspire **trust, loyalty,** and **mental well-being** in their teams, ensuring that firefighters are not only physically prepared for the challenges they face but mentally and emotionally equipped to handle the pressures of their profession.

By fostering a culture of **care, empathy,** and **support,** compassionate leaders create environments where firefighters can thrive, both in moments of crisis and in their long-term careers.

CHAPTER TWELVE

Preventing Burnout – Strategies for Sustainable Performance

Chapter 12: Preventing Burnout – Strategies for Sustainable Performance

The Cost of Burnout in the Fire Service

The fire service is demanding—physically, mentally, and emotionally. Firefighters are constantly exposed to high-stress situations, including traumatic incidents, long shifts, and unpredictable work environments. While the work is fulfilling, the demands can take a toll, leading to **burnout**. Burnout is more than just **exhaustion**; it's a state of emotional and physical depletion that can lead to **reduced performance, decreased morale**, and a **higher risk of mental health issues** such as depression, anxiety, and post-traumatic stress disorder (PTSD).

This chapter addresses the realities of burnout in the fire service and offers **practical strategies** for both **firefighters** and **leaders** to combat burnout and promote **sustainable performance**. By recognizing the signs of burnout early and implementing strategies to mitigate it, fire service professionals can continue to provide high-quality service while maintaining their **mental health** and **well-being.**

Understanding Burnout: Signs and Symptoms

Burnout is not something that happens overnight. It develops gradually, often going unnoticed until it has a significant impact on an individual's well-being and job performance. Understanding the signs of burnout is the first step in preventing it.

Common Signs of Burnout:

- **Physical and Emotional Exhaustion**: Feeling drained, tired, or fatigued even after rest. There may also be emotional exhaustion, where individuals feel mentally drained or overwhelmed by their responsibilities.

- **Reduced Performance**: A decline in job performance, including difficulty focusing, decision-making, and completing tasks efficiently.

- **Detachment**: Feeling emotionally detached or disconnected from work or coworkers. This can manifest as a lack of motivation or interest in one's duties.

- **Increased Cynicism or Negativity**: A negative attitude toward work, colleagues, or clients, often stemming from frustration or disillusionment.

- **Physical Symptoms**: Chronic headaches, sleep disturbances, gastrointestinal issues, or other health problems often associated with prolonged stress.

Recognizing these symptoms early is essential for preventing burnout from becoming a more serious issue. Firefighters experiencing these symptoms should seek support and employ **self-care** strategies before burnout significantly impacts their career and well-being.

The Causes of Burnout in the Fire Service

The causes of burnout in the fire service are multi-faceted, involving both external factors (such as the demands of the job) and internal factors (such as an individual's coping mechanisms). Understanding these causes is key to developing targeted strategies for preventing burnout.

External Factors Contributing to Burnout:

- **High Job Demands**: Firefighters regularly face long hours, high-pressure situations, and unpredictable shifts. The **physical** and **emotional demands** of the job can wear down even the most resilient individuals.

- **Trauma Exposure**: Constant exposure to traumatic events, including accidents, injuries, and fatalities, can lead to emotional fatigue and **secondary trauma**. The cumulative effect of these incidents can contribute significantly to burnout.

- **Lack of Support**: A lack of support from leadership, coworkers, or family can lead to feelings of isolation and increase the likelihood of burnout.

- **Organizational Stress**: Budget cuts, understaffing, and other organizational issues can create a stressful work environment, contributing to burnout.

Internal Factors Contributing to Burnout:

- **Perfectionism**: Firefighters who hold themselves to extremely high standards or feel the need to be perfect may experience greater stress and burnout. The pressure to perform flawlessly can be overwhelming.

- **Poor Coping Mechanisms**: Individuals who struggle with managing stress through healthy coping mechanisms are more susceptible to burnout. Relying on unhealthy behaviors such as substance abuse, denial, or isolation can exacerbate burnout.

- **Lack of Boundaries**: Firefighters who don't establish clear boundaries between work and personal life may struggle to maintain a healthy balance. When work becomes all-consuming, burnout is more likely.

Strategies for Preventing Burnout

Preventing burnout requires both **individual** and **organizational** efforts. Both firefighters and leadership must actively engage in **strategies** to maintain mental health and performance. These strategies can be broken down into several key areas: **self-care, resilience-building,** and **supportive leadership**.

Prioritize Self-Care

Self-care is a proactive approach to maintaining mental health and avoiding burnout. Firefighters must develop habits that prioritize their **physical, emotional,** and **psychological** well-being.

- **Physical Care**: Engage in regular exercise, eat a balanced diet, get enough sleep, and avoid unhealthy habits such as excessive caffeine or substance use.

- **Mental and Emotional Care**: Take time for hobbies,

relaxation, and activities that bring joy outside of work. Practice mindfulness or meditation to manage stress and improve mental clarity.

- **Social Support**: Build a strong support network of friends, family, and colleagues. Engaging in social activities and leaning on trusted individuals during tough times can alleviate stress.

By prioritizing self-care, firefighters can better manage the stresses of their job and reduce the likelihood of burnout.

Build Resilience

Resilience—the ability to bounce back from setbacks and maintain strength under stress—is a key factor in preventing burnout. Firefighters can build resilience by developing certain **mental skills** and **coping strategies**.

- **Mindfulness and Stress Management**: Mindfulness practices, such as deep breathing exercises and progressive muscle relaxation, can help reduce stress and maintain focus during challenging situations.

- **Positive Thinking**: Cultivate a positive mindset by focusing on achievements, practicing gratitude, and reframing negative thoughts.

- **Emotional Intelligence**: Developing emotional intelligence helps individuals understand and manage their emotions, as well as empathize with others, which can prevent emotional exhaustion.

Building resilience enables firefighters to recover from tough situations, adapt to stress, and maintain long-term well-being in their profession.

Supportive Leadership and Organizational Strategies

Leadership plays a crucial role in preventing burnout. Leaders who recognize the signs of burnout and actively support their team members can help reduce stress and promote a culture of well-being.

- **Encourage Time Off**: Leaders should encourage firefighters to take time off and disconnect from work to recharge. Adequate rest is essential for recovery and maintaining performance.

- **Provide Mental Health Resources**: Departments should offer access to mental health resources, including counseling services, stress management programs, and peer support groups.

- **Create a Supportive Work Environment**: Foster a culture of **open communication, mutual support**, and **empathy**. Encourage team members to check in with one another and provide assistance during tough times.

- **Provide Recognition and Appreciation**: Acknowledge the hard work and dedication of firefighters. Recognizing accomplishments, big or small, boosts morale and reinforces a sense of **purpose** and **value**.

Leadership should also model self-care and emotional well-being, setting an example for their team to follow.

Preventing Burnout: A Holistic Approach

Preventing burnout requires a **holistic approach**—one that considers the well-being of the individual firefighter, the support system within the department, and the leadership culture. By fostering a culture that values **mental health**, encourages **self-care**, and promotes **resilience**, the fire service can reduce the impact of burnout and help firefighters sustain their performance over the long term.

Implement a Comprehensive Wellness Program

A wellness program that addresses physical, mental, and emotional health is a proactive way to reduce burnout. These programs might include:

- **Physical fitness assessments** and training programs.
- **Mental health seminars** or workshops.

- **Peer support programs** that provide a safe space to talk about personal struggles.

- **Stress-relief activities** such as yoga, meditation, or recreational team-building events.

Develop a Long-Term Strategy for Sustainable Performance

Departments should develop a long-term strategy for sustainable performance that integrates the principles of self-care, resilience-building, and supportive leadership. This strategy should include:

- **Regular check-ins with team members** to assess their mental and emotional health.

- **Ongoing training** in stress management, emotional intelligence, and leadership.

- **Clear policies** around time off, mental health resources, and expectations regarding work-life balance.

Case Study: Preventing Burnout in Action

At a metropolitan fire department, leadership implemented a comprehensive wellness program that included **physical fitness training, mental health workshops,** and **peer support networks**. Firefighters were given time to attend wellness seminars, and the department held regular wellness check-ins to gauge how individuals were coping with the demands of the job.

As a result:

- **Burnout rates decreased** by 25% over the course of a year.

- Firefighters reported feeling more **supported** and **resilient**.

- The department saw a **reduction in turnover** and an **increase in job satisfaction**.

This example demonstrates how **proactive wellness programs** and **supportive leadership** can prevent burnout and promote **sustainable performance**.

Preventing Burnout – A Shared Responsibility

Burnout is a serious issue in the fire service, but it is not inevitable. Through proactive strategies focused on **self-care, resilience,** and **supportive leadership,** burnout can be prevented. Firefighters, leaders, and organizations must work together to create a culture of well-being that promotes **sustainable performance** and **mental health**.

By addressing burnout early and creating a supportive environment, the fire service can continue to provide the highest level of care to their communities, while ensuring the well-being of those who serve.

CHAPTER THIRTEEN

The Power of Reflection – Learning from the Past

Chapter 13: The Power of Reflection – Learning from the Past

The Importance of Reflective Practices in the Fire Service

In the fast-paced and high-pressure world of the fire service, there is little time to pause and reflect. However, the practice of **reflection** is crucial for personal growth, professional development, and improving the effectiveness of fire departments. Reflection allows individuals and teams to **learn from past experiences**, **identify areas for improvement**, and enhance **decision-making** and **problem-solving** skills.

This chapter explores the power of reflection, how it can be integrated into fire service practices, and the benefits it brings to both **mental health** and **performance**. Through structured reflection, fire service professionals can foster a culture of continuous improvement, improve resilience, and reduce the risk of burnout and **psychological distress**.

The Role of Reflection in Mental Health and Resilience

Reflection serves as a vital tool in **resilience-building**. In high-stress jobs like firefighting, there is often little time to process the emotional and psychological impact of traumatic experiences. Reflecting on these experiences allows individuals to gain perspective, reduce the emotional burden, and **improve emotional regulation**.

Mental Health Benefits of Reflection:

- **Emotional Processing**: Reflection helps fire service professionals process the emotional aspects of their work. By acknowledging and understanding emotions, they can reduce the chances of **emotional numbing** or **repression**, which often lead to **mental health issues** like PTSD.

- **Stress Relief**: Reflecting on stressful situations can help firefighters see challenges from a different perspective, thus reducing their perceived stress. Reflection fosters **self-awareness**, which allows individuals to understand their triggers and responses, helping them manage their emotions more effectively.

- **Improved Coping Strategies**: Through reflection,

firefighters can identify which coping strategies worked well in high-stress situations and which didn't, allowing them to develop healthier ways to handle future stressors.

By embedding reflection into daily routines and post-incident reviews, firefighters can develop stronger emotional resilience and improve their ability to handle future stress.

Reflection as a Tool for Performance Improvement

In addition to its mental health benefits, reflection plays a crucial role in improving the **performance** of individuals and teams. In the fire service, where split-second decisions can mean the difference between life and death, it's vital that firefighters learn from past incidents to refine their **decision-making, communication**, and **problem-solving** abilities.

Benefits of Reflective Practice for Performance:

- **Identifying Mistakes and Successes**: Reflection provides a space to evaluate what went right and what went wrong during an incident. By identifying mistakes, firefighters can learn to avoid repeating them in the future. At the same time, acknowledging successes reinforces effective behaviors and decision-making.

- **Enhancing Decision-Making**: Reflection enables individuals to **analyze the choices** they made during a critical incident, helping them assess their decision-making process. This reflection can lead to better **decision-making** under pressure, as individuals gain insight into their thought processes and develop a deeper understanding of their judgment.

- **Building Team Cohesion**: Reflecting on team dynamics during an incident can reveal communication strengths and weaknesses. Firefighters can learn how to better collaborate in high-stress environments, which ultimately leads to better teamwork and performance.

By making reflection a regular part of professional development, fire service professionals can continuously refine their skills and improve their overall effectiveness on the job.

Structured Reflection – Techniques for Firefighters and Leaders

While reflection is a powerful tool, it needs to be structured in order to be effective. Without guidance, reflection can become overly vague or surface-level. There are several structured techniques that can help firefighters and leaders reflect in a meaningful way.

Debriefing Sessions

Debriefing is a structured reflection process that occurs after an incident or shift. These sessions provide an opportunity for team members to **analyze** their performance, **discuss challenges**, and identify areas for improvement. Debriefing sessions should be **non-punitive** and encourage open communication and learning.

Key components of effective debriefing include:

- Reviewing the **goals** of the incident or shift.
- Analyzing what worked well and what didn't.
- Encouraging constructive feedback from all team members.
- **Action planning** for future improvement.

Journaling

Journaling is an individual reflective practice that allows firefighters to process their thoughts, emotions, and experiences. Writing down experiences can help individuals better understand their emotional reactions and gain clarity on how they can improve.

Firefighters can use journaling to:

- **Record their feelings** about particular incidents or situations.

- Reflect on what they did well and what could be improved.

- Develop **coping strategies** for dealing with future stressful situations.

Journaling provides a safe and private space to work through complex emotions and experiences.

After Action Reviews (AAR)

After Action Reviews (AARs) are formalized reflection processes that are often used after a significant event or operation. AARs are focused on **performance assessment** and **process improvement**. They are designed to help individuals and teams **identify lessons learned**, review **performance metrics**, and adjust strategies for future success.

The AAR process generally follows this format:

- **What was supposed to happen** versus **what actually happened**.

- **What went well** and **why**.

- **What can be improved** and **how**.

AARs help organizations create a continuous improvement cycle that builds on past experiences.

Creating a Culture of Reflection in the Fire Service

For reflection to be truly effective, it must be embedded into the **culture** of the fire service. Leaders must promote reflective practices as an integral part of the department's daily operations, rather than as a one-time activity.

Strategies for Encouraging Reflection:

- **Lead by Example**: Leaders should model reflective practices, such as engaging in debriefing sessions and sharing their own reflections on incidents. When leaders demonstrate the value of reflection, it encourages others to do the same.

- **Create Safe Spaces for Reflection**: Firefighters should feel comfortable reflecting without fear of judgment or retribution. Departments should foster an environment that encourages openness and trust.

- **Integrate Reflection into Training**: Incorporating reflection into training programs can help firefighters develop reflective habits early in their careers.

Training exercises, such as scenario-based simulations, should always include a **debriefing** and **reflection** component.

- **Regularly Schedule Reflection Time**: Make reflection a routine part of every shift or post-incident. Scheduling regular times for reflection ensures that it becomes a consistent practice rather than an afterthought.

By making reflection a regular and expected part of the fire service, leaders can enhance the mental health, resilience, and performance of their teams.

Case Study: Reflective Practice in Action

A fire department in a mid-sized city implemented a comprehensive **reflective practice program** as part of their commitment to improving firefighter well-being and performance. They began by incorporating daily debriefing sessions at the end of each shift, as well as weekly journaling sessions for firefighters to reflect on their experiences.

The results were striking:

- Firefighters reported feeling **more connected** to their work and their team.
- **Mental health issues**, including symptoms of PTSD,

decreased due to the emotional processing provided by reflection.

- The department saw an **increase in performance**, particularly in the areas of decision-making and teamwork during high-stress incidents.

This case study highlights the transformative power of reflective practices in the fire service and demonstrates how intentional reflection can lead to both improved **mental health** and **performance**.

The Ongoing Journey of Reflection

Reflection is not a one-time activity—it's an ongoing process that requires continuous engagement. For fire service professionals, integrating reflection into daily routines is essential for long-term success, mental health, and professional growth.

By making reflection a core part of their personal and professional development, firefighters can improve their ability to handle stress, learn from past experiences, and **enhance their resilience**. As they grow in their reflective practices, fire service leaders and teams will foster a culture of continuous improvement that ensures both individual and collective success in the face of adversity.

B.R.I.C.K. BY B.R.I.C.K.

CHAPTER FOURTEEN

Navigating Change – Embracing Adaptability in the Fire Service

Chapter 14: Navigating Change – Embracing Adaptability in the Fire Service

The Need for Adaptability in an Evolving Environment

In an era marked by constant **change**, the fire service must remain agile and adaptable to the evolving demands of society, technology, and the challenges of the modern world. The complexities of firefighting, emergency response, and public safety require fire service professionals to stay ahead of emerging trends, integrate new technologies, and adapt their approaches to effectively address a wide range of incidents.

However, change can often be perceived as a threat, particularly in environments with established norms, routines, and protocols. This chapter will explore the importance of **adaptability** in the fire service, focusing on the mental health benefits, leadership strategies, and practical techniques for embracing change. Navigating change is not only essential for maintaining high performance but also for promoting **resilience** and **well-being** among fire service personnel.

The Psychological Impact of Change on Firefighters

Change, while inevitable, often triggers stress and resistance. Firefighters, who work in high-stakes environments, may be particularly sensitive to shifts in routines, procedures, or the way their roles are perceived within the organization. The psychological impact of change can range from **anxiety** and **uncertainty** to frustration and burnout, especially when changes are perceived as threatening or poorly communicated.

Understanding the Emotional Response to Change:

- **Fear of the Unknown**: Change often brings uncertainty, and uncertainty can provoke fear. Fear of new technologies, altered workflows, or unfamiliar procedures may lead to hesitation, reluctance, or anxiety among firefighters.

- **Loss of Control**: Firefighters, who are trained to handle specific situations, may feel a loss of control when faced with significant changes in their environment. The sense of autonomy can be diminished if they feel their roles are being altered without their input.

- **Increased Stress**: Adapting to change requires energy, focus, and resilience. When these adjustments are frequent or poorly managed, they can contribute to **increased stress**, mental fatigue, and **emotional exhaustion**, especially if the changes affect well-being or job satisfaction.

Despite these challenges, embracing change and learning to adapt can ultimately foster resilience, promote mental health, and improve performance.

The Importance of Adaptability in Leadership

Fire service leaders play a pivotal role in guiding their teams through periods of change. Their ability to model adaptability, communicate effectively, and lead through uncertainty directly impacts how the rest of the department responds to challenges.

Leadership Strategies for Navigating Change:

- **Lead by Example**: Leaders who demonstrate **flexibility** and a positive attitude towards change set the tone for their teams. When leadership embraces new challenges with confidence and an open mind, it encourages others to do the same.

- **Transparent Communication**: One of the most effective ways to alleviate anxiety about change is to provide clear, transparent communication. Leaders should openly share the reasons for the change, the anticipated outcomes, and the support available to their team members.

- **Involvement and Input**: Involving firefighters in the change process helps them feel empowered and valued. Leaders can encourage feedback and suggestions from their teams to create a sense of ownership and control over the changes being implemented.

- **Support and Training**: Leaders should ensure that adequate support systems and training are in place to help firefighters adapt to new practices, technologies, or protocols. Offering continuous development opportunities helps employees feel more competent and confident in handling change.

Strong, adaptable leadership fosters a resilient and cohesive team that can thrive in the face of uncertainty.

Embracing Change Through Professional Development

One of the most powerful ways to embrace change is through **professional development**. Continuous learning allows fire service professionals to stay ahead of industry trends, enhance their skills, and cultivate a mindset of **growth** and **adaptability**.

Professional Development Opportunities for Firefighters:

- **Ongoing Training**: Firefighters should have access to regular training opportunities that cover both **new technologies** and **emergency response strategies**. Training ensures they stay prepared for evolving job demands and reinforces their sense of competence.

- **Cross-Training**: Exposure to a variety of roles and responsibilities within the fire department enables firefighters to develop a diverse skill set, fostering adaptability when changes in operations or technology occur.

- **Leadership Development**: For those aspiring to leadership roles, training in leadership principles and decision-making during times of change is essential. Developing strong leadership capabilities can equip future leaders with the skills needed to guide their teams through difficult transitions.

By prioritizing continuous learning and development, fire service professionals can feel more confident in their ability to adapt to changes and challenges.

Building Organizational Resilience Through Adaptability

The fire service, like any organization, must be resilient in the face of challenges. Organizational resilience refers to the **ability of a department** to adapt to and recover from setbacks, changes, and external pressures. A resilient fire department can **quickly pivot** in response to new circumstances while maintaining operational efficiency and personnel well-being.

Cultivating Resilience Through Adaptability:

- **Developing a Growth Mindset**: A growth mindset encourages individuals to view challenges as opportunities for learning and improvement, rather than threats. Fostering this mindset within the organization can help individuals respond more positively to change and **bounce back** more quickly from setbacks.

- **Encouraging Collaboration and Support**: A resilient

organization thrives on **collaboration** and mutual support. By promoting teamwork and a sense of community, fire departments can weather the challenges of change with collective strength and problem-solving capacity.

- **Fostering Flexibility in Processes**: Fire departments can enhance resilience by building flexibility into their operational processes. This flexibility enables teams to adjust to changes without sacrificing effectiveness or safety. Creating adaptable systems can mitigate the stress and frustration that often accompany changes.

An organization that prioritizes resilience and adaptability is better equipped to face the challenges of an ever-changing world.

Case Study: Adaptability in Action

A fire department in a rapidly growing metropolitan area faced significant challenges due to an influx of new technologies, increased demand for services, and a changing socio-economic landscape. The department recognized the need to embrace adaptability to meet these evolving demands.

To successfully navigate these changes, the department implemented several strategies:

- **Regular Training**: The department introduced a comprehensive training program focused on the integration of new technologies, including advanced firefighting equipment, drones for aerial surveillance, and **data-driven decision-making** tools.

- **Feedback Loops**: Leaders implemented regular feedback sessions, where firefighters were encouraged to share their concerns and suggestions about the changes. This open line of communication helped identify potential issues early and fostered a sense of ownership among the team.

- **Resilience Training**: The department introduced resilience training as part of their ongoing professional development, focusing on building mental and emotional resilience to cope with the stress of adapting to change.

As a result, the department successfully adapted to new demands, improved firefighter performance, and experienced a marked reduction in stress and burnout. The department's ability to embrace change led to increased operational efficiency and enhanced **mental health** for all personnel.

Thriving in Change

Adaptability is a critical skill for fire service professionals in a world that is constantly evolving. While change can be unsettling, it also provides opportunities for growth, development, and improvement. Firefighters and leaders who embrace change with a positive attitude and a commitment to continuous learning can navigate even the most challenging transitions with resilience.

By fostering an environment that values adaptability, communication, and support, fire departments can not only improve **performance** but also safeguard the **mental health** and well-being of their personnel. Change may be inevitable, but the way we approach it determines whether it will lead to growth or stagnation.

CHAPTER FIFTEEN

Cultivating Emotional Intelligence – Enhancing Interpersonal Skills in the Fire Service

Chapter 15: Cultivating Emotional Intelligence – Enhancing Interpersonal Skills in the Fire Service

The Role of Emotional Intelligence in Fire Service Leadership

In the high-pressure world of fire service, where rapid decision-making, teamwork, and crisis management are commonplace, emotional intelligence (EI) is often the differentiating factor between good and great leaders and responders. Emotional intelligence is the ability to recognize, understand, and manage our own emotions, as well as recognize, understand, and influence the emotions of others.

For fire service personnel, EI is critical for building effective teams, reducing stress, improving communication, and ensuring positive mental health outcomes. This chapter explores the importance of emotional intelligence in fire service leadership and provides actionable strategies to develop and enhance these interpersonal skills. By cultivating emotional intelligence, fire service leaders and teams can navigate the demands of their profession with greater empathy, resilience, and success.

The Five Components of Emotional Intelligence

Emotional intelligence is a multifaceted skill set that encompasses several core components. Each of these components plays a vital role in fostering positive relationships, enhancing decision-making, and improving overall performance in the fire service.

Self-Awareness

Self-awareness is the ability to recognize and understand your own emotions and their effect on your behavior and decision-making. Fire service personnel who are self-aware are able to manage their reactions in high-stress situations, avoid burnout, and maintain a clear focus on the mission.

- **Benefits of Self-Awareness**: Enhances decision-making under pressure, reduces emotional reactivity, and improves mental health by helping individuals identify triggers and manage stress effectively.

- **Practical Application**: Firefighters can use self-awareness to monitor their emotional states during stressful calls or training exercises, ensuring that they stay focused and maintain control.

Self-Regulation

Self-regulation is the ability to control or redirect disruptive emotions and impulses. In the context of firefighting, self-regulation is essential for maintaining calm under pressure, preventing rash decisions, and ensuring safety for oneself and others.

- **Benefits of Self-Regulation**: Promotes resilience, reduces emotional outbursts, and fosters a composed, thoughtful approach to problem-solving in critical situations.

- **Practical Application**: A firefighter might practice self-regulation by taking a deep breath or pausing before reacting during a tense emergency scene, allowing for a more measured response.

Motivation

Motivation refers to the inner drive to achieve goals for reasons beyond external rewards or recognition. In the fire service, motivation often stems from a sense of duty, service to the community, and the desire to protect others.

- **Benefits of Motivation**: Encourages perseverance in challenging circumstances, fosters a strong sense of purpose, and helps combat burnout.

- **Practical Application**: Firefighters can align their personal values with the mission of the department, staying motivated even in the face of adversity or difficult situations.

Empathy

Empathy is the ability to understand and share the feelings of others. In the fire service, empathy is crucial for building rapport with teammates, victims, and their families. It allows firefighters to provide compassionate care and support during emotionally charged situations.

- **Benefits of Empathy**: Builds trust, strengthens relationships, and improves communication, leading to better team dynamics and patient care.

- **Practical Application**: Empathy can be practiced by actively listening to colleagues and victims, offering words of encouragement, or providing emotional support during critical incidents.

Social Skills

Social skills involve the ability to manage relationships

and navigate social complexities. In the fire service, strong social skills are essential for effective communication, teamwork, and conflict resolution.

- **Benefits of Social Skills**: Facilitates collaboration, reduces misunderstandings, and strengthens team cohesion, ultimately leading to more efficient and effective responses.

- **Practical Application**: Firefighters can develop social skills by actively participating in team-building activities, practicing conflict resolution techniques, and ensuring open communication with both team members and leadership.

The Impact of Emotional Intelligence on Fire Service Performance

Fire service professionals are routinely placed in situations that require both **mental clarity** and **emotional control**. When emotional intelligence is lacking, it can negatively affect decision-making, team dynamics, and the ability to handle stress. Leaders who fail to recognize the emotional states of their team or their own emotional responses may exacerbate conflicts, reduce morale, and increase the likelihood of mental health issues.

Enhancing Communication and Teamwork

Effective communication is a cornerstone of successful fire service operations. Emotional intelligence enhances communication by allowing firefighters and leaders to interpret and respond to emotional cues from others, whether it's a distressed colleague or a panicked victim.

- **Example**: A leader who is attuned to the emotional state of their team can provide reassurance during a stressful call, thus improving coordination and maintaining focus.

- **Teamwork**: High EI helps to build teams that are not only skilled but also emotionally attuned to one another, allowing them to collaborate more effectively under pressure.

Reducing Stress and Preventing Burnout

Firefighters often face situations that are physically and emotionally demanding, leading to high levels of stress. Emotional intelligence equips individuals with the tools to manage stress, regulate emotional reactions, and avoid burnout. Teams with high EI are also better equipped to support one another, creating a protective buffer against stress and mental exhaustion.

- **Example**: A firefighter experiencing stress may be

able to recognize their emotional state and use techniques such as deep breathing or seeking support from teammates to regain composure.

- **Burnout Prevention**: EI also enables leaders to spot early signs of burnout in team members and intervene proactively by offering support or adjusting workloads to reduce stress.

Decision-Making in High-Pressure Situations

Firefighters often must make life-or-death decisions in high-pressure, high-stakes environments. The ability to manage one's emotions and stay clear-headed is critical to making informed, effective decisions that prioritize safety and success.

- **Example**: During a complex rescue operation, a firefighter with high EI will be able to remain calm and make logical decisions, even in the face of intense stress, while considering both tactical options and emotional factors (such as the needs of victims or teammates).

Building Emotional Intelligence in the Fire Service

While some individuals may naturally possess strong emotional intelligence, it is a skill that can be developed and enhanced through practice. Fire service leaders and personnel should prioritize EI development as part of their ongoing professional growth.

EI Training for Firefighters

Training programs that focus on emotional intelligence can help fire service personnel develop self-awareness, self-regulation, empathy, and social skills. These programs should be integrated into regular professional development activities and tailored to the unique challenges faced by firefighters.

- **Example**: Training programs might include role-playing exercises that simulate high-stress situations, helping individuals practice empathy, self-regulation, and communication in realistic scenarios.

Creating a Supportive Environment

Fire departments can foster emotional intelligence by creating a supportive work environment that encourages open communication, peer support, and emotional well-being. Leaders should set the tone by modeling EI skills and supporting their teams in developing these competencies.

- **Example**: Implementing mentorship programs, peer counseling, and team-building exercises can help foster an emotionally intelligent culture within the department.

Case Study: Emotional Intelligence in Action

A fire department faced a significant challenge when a fire caused a collapse, trapping several victims inside a building. In this chaotic and high-stress situation, emotional intelligence played a crucial role in the successful rescue operation.

Firefighters displayed the following EI skills:

- **Self-Regulation**: Despite the intense pressure, firefighters remained composed, managing their emotions and staying focused on the task at hand.

- **Empathy**: The team communicated effectively with victims, offering reassurance and emotional support while ensuring the safety of everyone involved.

- **Social Skills**: The team worked collaboratively, sharing information and coordinating efforts seamlessly.

In the aftermath of the incident, the department recognized the importance of EI in ensuring both operational success and the mental well-being of the team. This event prompted the implementation of EI-focused training, resulting in improved team dynamics and performance in subsequent operations.

The Power of Emotional Intelligence

Emotional intelligence is an essential skill set for fire service professionals. From improving communication and teamwork to reducing stress and preventing burnout, EI plays a critical role in both the mental health of firefighters and the success of fire service operations. By cultivating emotional intelligence, fire service personnel can enhance their leadership abilities, improve their interpersonal relationships, and ensure the well-being of both themselves and those they serve.

CHAPTER SIXTEEN

The Fire Service and Mental Health – Breaking the Stigma and Supporting Well-Being

Chapter 16: The Fire Service and Mental Health – Breaking the Stigma and Supporting Well-Being

The Silent Crisis in the Fire Service

The fire service is often seen as a pillar of strength, courage, and resilience. Firefighters are the ones who rush into burning buildings, risk their lives to save others, and face intense physical and mental challenges on a daily basis. However, the mental health struggles of firefighters are frequently overlooked or minimized. The stigma surrounding mental health issues in the fire service often prevents individuals from seeking the help they need, which can lead to long-term psychological damage, burnout, and even suicide.

Mental health is just as important as physical health, and it is essential that the fire service breaks the silence surrounding mental health issues. By fostering a culture of support, openness, and understanding, fire service leaders can not only help individuals cope with the emotional toll of their profession but also improve team dynamics, job satisfaction, and overall resilience.

This chapter explores the mental health challenges faced by firefighters, the stigma that often prevents them from seeking help, and the strategies that fire service organizations can implement to support the mental well-being of their personnel.

The Mental Health Challenges of Firefighters

Firefighters are regularly exposed to traumatic and stressful situations, which can have a significant impact on their mental health. The constant exposure to death, injury, and destruction can lead to a range of mental health issues, including post-traumatic stress disorder (PTSD), depression, anxiety, and substance abuse.

Post-Traumatic Stress Disorder (PTSD)

PTSD is one of the most common mental health conditions affecting firefighters. The repeated exposure to traumatic events, such as fatal fires, serious accidents, and violent incidents, can lead to intrusive memories, flashbacks, nightmares, and emotional numbness. The trauma experienced on the job can create lasting psychological scars that affect both personal and professional life.

- **Impact of PTSD**: Firefighters with PTSD may experience difficulty sleeping, irritability, difficulty concentrating, and emotional detachment. In some cases, untreated PTSD can lead to self-destructive behaviors, such as substance abuse or suicidal thoughts.

Depression and Anxiety

The emotional toll of the fire service, combined with the physical demands, can contribute to feelings of depression and anxiety. Long hours, exposure to traumatic incidents, and the stress of making life-and-death decisions can wear on firefighters' mental well-being. Feelings of sadness, hopelessness, and chronic worry can prevent individuals from performing at their best and lead to burnout.

- **Impact of Depression and Anxiety**: Firefighters suffering from depression or anxiety may find it difficult to cope with the demands of the job, leading to impaired decision-making, diminished performance, and a reduced ability to connect with colleagues and the public.

Substance Abuse

Substance abuse is a common coping mechanism among individuals in high-stress professions, including firefighters. Some firefighters may turn to alcohol or drugs to numb the pain of traumatic experiences or to manage stress. While this may offer temporary relief, it often exacerbates mental health problems and can lead to addiction and other serious consequences.

- **Impact of Substance Abuse**: Substance abuse in the fire service can impair judgment, reduce physical performance, and lead to interpersonal issues within the team. It also increases the risk of developing long-term physical and mental health issues.

The Stigma of Mental Health in the Fire Service

Despite the prevalence of mental health issues among firefighters, there is still a strong stigma associated with seeking help. The fire service has a culture that values strength, resilience, and bravery. Admitting to struggling mentally or emotionally is often perceived as a sign of weakness, and firefighters may fear judgment or retaliation if they disclose their mental health concerns.

The "Tough Guy" Mentality

The traditional "tough guy" mentality in the fire service encourages individuals to suppress their emotions and avoid seeking help. Firefighters are expected to be strong, self-reliant, and unflappable in the face of danger. As a result, mental health issues are often minimized, and individuals who express vulnerability are seen as less capable or competent.

- **Challenges**: This mentality can prevent firefighters from accessing the support they need, leading to untreated mental health issues that can affect their performance, relationships, and overall well-being.

Fear of Career Consequences

Many firefighters fear that acknowledging mental health struggles will negatively impact their careers. They may worry that seeking help will result in disciplinary action, a loss of their job, or reduced opportunities for advancement. This fear of stigma and retaliation can prevent individuals from reaching out for help, exacerbating the mental health crisis in the fire service.

- **Consequences of Silence**: When firefighters don't seek help due to fear of negative consequences, they are more likely to suffer in silence, which can worsen their condition and ultimately affect their ability to perform their duties effectively.

Strategies for Supporting Mental Health in the Fire Service

To address the mental health challenges faced by firefighters and reduce the stigma surrounding mental health, fire service organizations must take proactive steps to create a supportive environment that encourages open dialogue, provides resources, and prioritizes mental well-being.

Normalizing Conversations About Mental Health

The first step in breaking the stigma surrounding mental health is to normalize conversations about it. Fire service leaders should actively encourage discussions about mental health and emotional well-being, making it clear that it is acceptable to talk about struggles and seek help when needed.

- **Practical Strategies**: Leaders can incorporate mental health discussions into training sessions, team meetings, and wellness programs. They can also share their own experiences and struggles to model vulnerability and openness.

Providing Mental Health Resources

Fire departments should provide easy access to mental health resources, including counseling services, peer support programs, and confidential hotlines. These resources should be available to firefighters both on and off duty and should be tailored to the unique challenges faced by fire service personnel.

- **Practical Strategies**: Offering Employee Assistance Programs (EAPs), creating partnerships with mental health professionals, and providing access to mental health days can help firefighters manage their well-being.

Building a Culture of Peer Support

Peer support programs are an effective way to address mental health in the fire service. These programs connect firefighters with trained peers who can offer guidance, support, and a listening ear. Peer support provides a safe, non-judgmental environment where firefighters can share their concerns and seek help without fear of stigma.

- **Practical Strategies**: Establishing formal peer support programs, where trained individuals are available to assist their colleagues, can create a more supportive and connected culture within the fire service.

Providing Training on Mental Health Awareness

Training on mental health awareness should be incorporated into fire service education and ongoing professional development. Firefighters should be equipped with the tools to recognize the signs of mental health struggles in themselves and their colleagues. Training should also include coping strategies for managing stress and maintaining emotional well-being.

- **Practical Strategies**: Including mental health first aid training, stress management techniques, and resilience-building exercises as part of standard fire service training can help normalize mental health care and reduce stigma.

Case Study: Mental Health Support in Action

In one fire department, leadership took proactive steps to address the mental health needs of their personnel by implementing a comprehensive mental health and wellness program. This program included mental health awareness training, access to peer support programs, and confidential counseling services. As a result, the department saw a significant reduction in stress-related issues, improved team dynamics, and better overall job satisfaction.

In one instance, a firefighter who had been struggling with PTSD reached out to a peer support mentor. With the support of the program, the firefighter was able to receive counseling and gradually return to work. The success of this program not only improved the mental health of individual firefighters but also fostered a culture of openness and support within the department.

Prioritizing Mental Health in the Fire Service

Mental health is a critical issue in the fire service that cannot be ignored. Firefighters face unique challenges that can take a significant toll on their mental well-being. By breaking the stigma surrounding mental health, normalizing conversations, providing access to resources, and building a culture of peer support, fire service organizations can ensure that their personnel are supported, resilient, and able to perform at their best.

It's time to prioritize the mental health of our firefighters and ensure they have the tools and support they need to succeed both on the job and in their personal lives.

CHAPTER SEVENTEEN

Building Resilience in Fire Service Personnel – The Power of Mental Toughness

Chapter 17: Building Resilience in Fire Service Personnel – The Power of Mental Toughness

Resilience – The Key to Thriving in the Fire Service

The fire service is one of the most demanding professions, requiring physical strength, mental sharpness, and the ability to perform under extreme pressure. Resilience, the ability to adapt to stress and bounce back from adversity, is a crucial trait that enables firefighters to handle the many challenges they face. While physical training is vital for preparing firefighters to handle the physical demands of the job, building mental resilience is equally important for ensuring they are able to cope with the emotional and psychological stress that comes with the job.

Mental toughness—the ability to maintain focus, composure, and determination even under the most challenging circumstances—is a key component of resilience. Fire service personnel face life-threatening situations, witness traumatic events, and make difficult decisions regularly. Without the mental strength to navigate these challenges, firefighters risk burnout, trauma, and impaired performance.

This chapter delves into the importance of building resilience in fire service personnel, explores strategies for developing mental toughness, and highlights the impact of resilient leadership on the well-being of individuals and the organization as a whole.

Understanding Resilience in the Fire Service

Resilience is the capacity to recover from difficulties and adapt positively to adversity. In the fire service, resilience enables firefighters to maintain their emotional stability, work effectively in high-stress environments, and recover from traumatic events. It's not about being immune to stress or trauma, but rather about developing the skills and mindset to overcome challenges without letting them overwhelm you.

The Emotional Toll of the Fire Service

Firefighters experience high levels of stress due to the unpredictable nature of their work. Whether it's responding to a fire, rescuing someone from a dangerous situation, or dealing with the aftermath of a traumatic event, firefighters often operate in emotionally charged environments. The constant exposure to life-and-death situations can take a toll on their emotional and psychological well-being.

- **Impact of Emotional Stress**: Chronic exposure to stress and trauma can lead to burnout, anxiety, depression, PTSD, and other mental health challenges. Resilience helps firefighters cope with the emotional toll of their work and continue to perform effectively.

The Importance of Mental Toughness

Mental toughness is the ability to persevere through adversity and remain focused, even when faced with uncertainty, fear, or pressure. In the fire service, mental toughness is essential for overcoming obstacles and performing effectively in high-pressure situations. It allows firefighters to stay calm under pressure, make sound decisions, and continue working despite difficult circumstances.

- **The Role of Mental Toughness**: Firefighters with mental toughness are more likely to remain focused during crises, recover quickly from setbacks, and maintain a positive outlook, all of which contribute to their overall resilience.

Building Resilience in Fire Service Personnel

Resilience is not something that firefighters are born with; it's a skill that can be developed over time. By incorporating resilience-building strategies into their training and daily routines, fire service personnel can strengthen their ability to cope with the stresses of the job and perform at their best, even in the most challenging situations.

Strengthening Emotional Awareness and Regulation

One of the key aspects of resilience is emotional awareness—the ability to recognize and understand your emotions in the moment. Emotional regulation involves managing those emotions effectively, especially when under stress. Firefighters who can regulate their emotions are better equipped to handle high-pressure situations and avoid being overwhelmed by negative feelings such as fear, frustration, or anger.

- **Practical Strategies**: Firefighters can practice mindfulness and emotional awareness exercises, such as deep breathing or meditation, to enhance emotional regulation. Additionally, they can be taught how to identify and reframe negative thoughts to build a more positive and resilient mindset.

-

Developing a Growth Mindset

A growth mindset is the belief that abilities and intelligence can be developed through hard work, perseverance, and learning. Firefighters with a growth mindset are more likely to view challenges as opportunities for growth, rather than as insurmountable obstacles. They embrace failure as part of the learning process and are not deterred by setbacks.

- **Practical Strategies**: Firefighters can be encouraged to set small, achievable goals, focus on progress rather than perfection, and view difficult situations as opportunities for growth and development. Acknowledging and celebrating small victories can help reinforce a growth mindset.

Enhancing Physical Fitness and Self-Care

Physical fitness plays a crucial role in building resilience. The physical demands of firefighting require firefighters to be in peak physical condition, but maintaining physical health also has a significant impact on mental well-being. Regular exercise improves mood, reduces stress, and increases energy levels—all of which contribute to greater resilience.

- **Practical Strategies**: Fire departments can promote

physical fitness by offering access to fitness programs, providing time for exercise during shifts, and encouraging healthy eating habits. Additionally, self-care routines, such as adequate sleep, nutrition, and relaxation, should be emphasized as part of a firefighter's overall resilience plan.

Fostering Social Connections and Support

Social support is one of the most important factors in building resilience. Firefighters who have strong social connections—both within their department and outside of it—are better able to cope with stress and trauma. Peer support, in particular, plays a critical role in helping firefighters process their emotions and share experiences in a safe and supportive environment.

- **Practical Strategies**: Creating peer support networks within the fire department, fostering camaraderie through team-building exercises, and providing opportunities for firefighters to connect with others can strengthen resilience. Encouraging open communication and offering safe spaces for discussing mental health can also help break the stigma surrounding mental well-being.

Resilient Leadership in the Fire Service

Resilient leadership is critical to fostering a culture of resilience within the fire service. Leaders who demonstrate mental toughness, emotional intelligence, and a growth mindset set the tone for the entire department. By prioritizing resilience and creating a supportive environment, leaders can help their personnel thrive in the face of adversity.

Leading by Example

Resilient leaders model the behaviors they wish to see in their personnel. When leaders demonstrate mental toughness, emotional regulation, and a positive attitude, they set a powerful example for others to follow. By openly discussing challenges and showing vulnerability, leaders can create an environment where it's acceptable to seek help and prioritize mental health.

- **Practical Strategies**: Fire service leaders can engage in resilience-building practices themselves, such as physical fitness, mindfulness, and stress management, and share their personal experiences with their teams. Leaders can also encourage regular check-ins and provide mental health resources for their personnel.

Promoting a Culture of Well-Being

A resilient fire service culture is one where well-being is prioritized, and mental health is seen as an integral part of overall performance. Leaders can implement policies and initiatives that support mental health, such as access to counseling services, peer support programs, and mental health awareness training. Additionally, promoting work-life balance and fostering an environment of trust and transparency can help create a healthier work culture.

- **Practical Strategies**: Fire service leaders can advocate for mental health days, provide training on stress management, and ensure that personnel are not overworked or fatigued. Creating a workplace that values mental and emotional well-being is essential for building resilience.

The Power of Resilience in the Fire Service

Building resilience in fire service personnel is essential for ensuring their well-being, performance, and long-term success. Resilience allows firefighters to cope with the emotional and psychological stressors of their profession and to remain effective in their work. By developing mental toughness, fostering emotional regulation, promoting social support, and practicing self-care, firefighters can strengthen their resilience and thrive under pressure.

Resilient leadership plays a vital role in creating a supportive environment where mental health is prioritized, and firefighters feel empowered to seek help when needed. As fire service organizations continue to recognize the importance of resilience, they will not only improve the well-being of their personnel but also enhance the effectiveness and success of the entire team.

Building resilience is a journey, but with the right tools, strategies, and leadership, fire service personnel can weather any storm and come out stronger on the other side.

CHAPTER EIGHTEEN

The Role of Leadership in Building a Resilient Fire Service Culture

Chapter 18: The Role of Leadership in Building a Resilient Fire Service Culture

The Influence of Leadership on Organizational Resilience

Leadership is the cornerstone of any resilient organization, and in the fire service, resilient leadership is the foundation upon which a strong and supportive fire service culture is built. The demands of the profession are unique, and the mental, physical, and emotional challenges firefighters face require leaders who understand how to guide their personnel through adversity. A resilient fire service culture is not created by accident; it is cultivated through deliberate leadership practices that foster well-being, promote emotional intelligence, and prioritize mental health.

This chapter explores the critical role leadership plays in fostering a resilient fire service culture. It emphasizes that the actions, attitudes, and behaviors of fire service leaders set the tone for the entire organization. Leaders must not only understand the importance of resilience but also actively nurture it through their decisions, actions, and support systems. When leadership prioritizes resilience, it enhances the ability of firefighters to perform at their best, supports their mental well-being, and ensures long-term success both individually and organizationally.

The Resilient Leader: Leading by Example

The first step in building a resilient fire service culture is for leaders to lead by example. Resilient leadership is not about simply issuing commands or delegating tasks—it's about modeling the behaviors and attitudes that are expected of others. When leaders display mental toughness, emotional regulation, and a positive outlook, they create a ripple effect throughout the organization.

The Power of Vulnerability

Resilient leaders understand the importance of vulnerability. They acknowledge their own struggles, weaknesses, and challenges, and by doing so, they create an environment where their personnel feel safe to do the same. This openness helps to break the stigma surrounding mental health and mental toughness, allowing firefighters to seek help when needed without fear of judgment or negative repercussions.

- **Practical Strategies**: Fire service leaders can set an example by discussing their own experiences with stress, trauma, or difficult situations. Sharing personal stories can humanize leaders and make them more relatable to their personnel. When leaders express their emotions in a healthy way, it encourages others to do the same.

Demonstrating Emotional Intelligence

Emotional intelligence (EI) is a vital skill for resilient leadership. EI involves the ability to recognize and manage one's own emotions, as well as the emotions of others. Fire service leaders with high emotional intelligence can better support their teams during stressful situations and help them process their feelings in healthy ways. By displaying empathy, self-regulation, and social awareness, leaders can build trust and foster an emotionally supportive environment.

- **Practical Strategies**: Leaders can enhance their emotional intelligence through training and self-reflection. Practicing active listening, validating others' emotions, and offering emotional support during challenging times are key strategies that leaders can employ to demonstrate EI.

Creating a Supportive and Transparent Environment

A resilient fire service culture thrives in an environment where openness, trust, and communication are prioritized. Fire service leaders must ensure that their personnel feel supported, not just professionally but emotionally as well. When there is transparency in decision-making, clear communication, and trust within the organization, firefighters are more likely to feel valued, respected, and motivated.

Promoting Open Communication

Effective communication is critical in high-stress professions like firefighting. Firefighters need to be able to communicate clearly and efficiently, especially in emergency situations. However, leaders also need to create a culture where open dialogue about mental health, stress, and emotional well-being is encouraged. This requires leaders to be approachable and non-judgmental.

- **Practical Strategies**: Leaders can promote open communication by holding regular team meetings, encouraging feedback, and fostering a culture where personnel feel safe to voice their concerns. Providing channels for confidential communication, such as counseling services or peer support networks, can also help employees feel supported.

Encouraging Collaboration and Teamwork

In the fire service, no one succeeds alone. Resilience is often built through collaboration and shared experiences. Leaders must foster a sense of camaraderie and teamwork within their departments to ensure that personnel feel connected and supported by their peers. Strong social support networks within the organization are a key factor in helping individuals bounce back from challenges.

- **Practical Strategies**: Leaders can promote teamwork through team-building exercises, collaborative training sessions, and encouraging social bonding outside of work. They should also ensure that no one feels isolated by encouraging inclusivity and offering support to those who may be struggling.

Prioritizing Mental Health and Well-Being

Resilient leadership is deeply connected to mental health advocacy. Leaders must make mental health a priority, ensuring that personnel have access to the resources, support systems, and tools they need to thrive. Building a fire service culture where mental health is treated with the same importance as physical health is essential for fostering long-term resilience.

Providing Mental Health Resources and Support

Leaders should ensure that mental health resources are readily available and easily accessible to their personnel. This can include offering access to counseling services, mental health awareness programs, and peer support networks. Leaders must also ensure that their personnel feel comfortable seeking help without the fear of stigma or reprisal.

- **Practical Strategies**: Leaders can advocate for mental health initiatives within the department, provide regular mental health check-ins, and encourage personnel to seek help when needed. Establishing partnerships with mental health professionals and providing resources such as confidential counseling or mental health hotlines can offer much-needed support.

Creating a Work-Life Balance

Fire service personnel often work long hours, face physically demanding tasks, and experience intense emotional stress. Leaders must understand the importance of work-life balance in promoting resilience. By encouraging personnel to take time off, use vacation days, and engage in self-care, leaders can help prevent burnout and maintain overall well-being.

- **Practical Strategies**: Leaders can implement policies that promote work-life balance, such as flexible scheduling, mandatory rest periods, and support for family needs. Encouraging regular breaks, time off, and healthy boundaries between work and personal life are essential for sustaining resilience in the long term.

Leadership Development: Fostering Future Resilient Leaders

Resilient leadership is not just about individual behaviors; it's about creating an organizational structure that cultivates future leaders who are equipped to handle the demands of the fire service. Leaders must invest in leadership development programs to ensure that upcoming generations of firefighters are prepared to lead with resilience, empathy, and effectiveness.

Mentorship and Development

Mentoring future leaders is a key responsibility for current fire service leaders. Resilient leaders understand the importance of developing the next generation of leaders by providing guidance, support, and opportunities for growth. Mentorship programs can help nurture leadership qualities such as emotional intelligence, decision-making, and communication skills.

- **Practical Strategies**: Fire service leaders can implement formal mentorship programs where experienced personnel guide and support newer members of the team. These programs can focus on both technical skills and leadership qualities, ensuring that future leaders are well-rounded and capable of building resilience in their own teams.

Training in Resilience Skills

Resilience training should be an integral part of leadership development. Leaders must be equipped with the tools, knowledge, and strategies to foster resilience within their teams. This includes training in stress management, conflict resolution, emotional regulation, and communication. By offering resilience training, leaders can build a more resilient workforce that can handle the inevitable challenges of the fire service.

- **Practical Strategies**: Leaders can implement regular resilience training sessions for themselves and their teams, focusing on practical skills for managing stress, handling trauma, and building mental toughness. This ensures that resilience becomes a core competency in the fire service.

Transforming Fire Service Culture Through Resilient Leadership

The role of leadership in building a resilient fire service culture cannot be overstated. Leaders are responsible for setting the tone, creating an environment of trust and support, and modeling the behaviors that contribute to organizational resilience. By prioritizing mental health, fostering teamwork, leading by example, and developing future leaders, resilient fire service leaders can build a culture that supports personnel both mentally and emotionally, allowing them to thrive despite the challenges they face.

As fire service leaders, it is our duty to ensure that the resilience of our personnel is as important as the physical training they receive. In doing so, we create a fire service culture that not only survives adversity but rises above it, emerging stronger and more unified.

CHAPTER NINETEEN

Leading with Empathy and Compassion

Chapter 19: Leading with Empathy and Compassion

The Power of Empathy in Leadership

In a profession as high-stress and physically demanding as the fire service, leadership goes beyond technical expertise and decision-making. True leadership is defined by emotional intelligence, particularly the capacity for empathy and compassion. Firefighters are not robots; they are human beings with emotions, mental health struggles, and personal lives that often intersect with their professional challenges. Leaders who approach their roles with empathy and compassion can transform an organization, fostering trust, respect, and a culture where personnel feel valued and understood.

Empathy is the ability to understand and share the feelings of others, while compassion is the willingness to act on that understanding to alleviate suffering. In the fire service, these qualities are vital in supporting personnel's mental health, strengthening team dynamics, and ensuring that the workforce remains resilient even in the face of tremendous adversity.

The Role of Empathy in Fire Service Leadership

Empathy is often seen as a "soft skill" in leadership, but it is one of the most critical factors in developing a supportive and resilient fire service culture. An empathetic leader can recognize when a team member is struggling, whether due to personal issues or job-related stress, and respond in a way that shows understanding and support. This connection creates an environment where personnel feel safe, respected, and empowered to seek help when needed.

Understanding the Emotional Needs of Firefighters

Firefighters regularly face traumatic events, long hours, and unpredictable situations. It is crucial that leaders are attuned to the emotional needs of their personnel. By acknowledging the emotional toll that the job can take, leaders can create a supportive environment that promotes healing and mental wellness.

- **Practical Strategies**: Leaders can actively listen to their team members, validate their experiences, and create opportunities for open discussions about emotional well-being. Regular check-ins with personnel, where leaders ask how they're feeling and offer a space to discuss personal or professional struggles, can go a long way in fostering emotional safety.

Active Listening: The Heart of Empathetic Leadership

Empathy in leadership starts with active listening. It's not just about hearing the words being spoken, but about fully understanding the emotions and intentions behind them. When leaders practice active listening, they not only gain a deeper understanding of their team members but also show that their thoughts and feelings are valued.

- **Practical Strategies**: Fire service leaders can practice active listening by making eye contact, not interrupting, and responding with empathy. Reflecting back what the person has said to ensure understanding and offering verbal or non-verbal cues to show engagement will create stronger connections with team members.

Compassion: Taking Action to Support Firefighters

While empathy involves understanding others' emotions, compassion involves taking that understanding and translating it into action. In the fire service, compassion manifests as leaders taking proactive steps to support their personnel during times of stress or difficulty. This could involve offering mental health resources, providing time off, or simply being present to listen and offer guidance.

Supporting Mental Health and Well-Being

Compassionate leaders are not only aware of their personnel's struggles but actively seek solutions that promote their well-being. Leaders who encourage mental health resources, create opportunities for decompression, and advocate for mental wellness programs contribute to a culture where mental health is prioritized and accepted.

- **Practical Strategies**: Fire service leaders can provide access to counseling services, create peer support networks, and actively promote mental health days. Encouraging personnel to take care of their mental health, just as they would their physical health, reinforces the importance of well-being in the fire service.

Promoting Work-Life Balance

A compassionate leader understands that firefighters are people with families, personal commitments, and needs outside of work. Promoting work-life balance helps to reduce burnout, stress, and fatigue—factors that can negatively impact mental health. Leaders should ensure that their personnel are not overburdened with shifts and are given ample time to rest and recover between calls.

- **Practical Strategies**: Leaders can implement scheduling policies that allow for adequate rest and time off. Encouraging personnel to take breaks, vacation days, and time to recharge will prevent burnout and improve overall job satisfaction.

Compassionate Leadership in Action

Compassionate leadership is not just about providing resources or allowing time off—it's about showing genuine care for the well-being of personnel. It requires leaders to be present, engaged, and attuned to the needs of their team. A compassionate leader fosters trust, improves morale, and strengthens the fire service organization as a whole.

Being Present During Difficult Times

Compassionate leaders show up when it matters most. Whether it's offering a listening ear during a difficult call, supporting someone who has lost a loved one, or helping a firefighter through a mental health crisis, compassionate leadership is about being present. Firefighters who feel supported during difficult times are more likely to stay engaged, committed, and productive.

- **Practical Strategies**: Leaders can be present by

attending critical incident debriefings, offering one-on-one support to personnel in need, and showing up at funerals or memorial services for fallen comrades. Their presence demonstrates to the team that they are valued and cared for.

Recognizing the Value of Personal Connections

A compassionate leader understands that work is only one part of a firefighter's life. Building personal relationships with team members creates a sense of belonging and strengthens trust. When firefighters know that their leaders care about them as individuals, they are more likely to be motivated, engaged, and resilient.

- **Practical Strategies**: Leaders can invest time in building personal relationships with their team members. Simple actions like remembering birthdays, offering congratulations for personal achievements, and taking an interest in their well-being outside of work contribute to a culture of compassion.

Creating a Compassionate Organizational Culture

Leadership sets the tone for the entire organization. When leaders demonstrate empathy and compassion, they lay the foundation for a fire service culture where these values are ingrained in the organization's fabric. Firefighters who work in an environment of compassion are more likely to feel supported, connected, and motivated to do their best work.

Cultivating a Culture of Compassion

Compassion should not be limited to leaders alone; it should permeate the entire fire service organization. Leaders must model compassionate behavior, but they must also encourage their personnel to do the same. Fostering a culture of compassion creates a workplace where firefighters support one another, share experiences, and collaborate to improve mental health and well-being.

- **Practical Strategies**: Leaders can implement training programs on emotional intelligence and empathy, promote team-building exercises, and provide opportunities for personnel to share experiences. Encouraging peer support networks, where firefighters can offer help and guidance to one another, will strengthen the organization's compassionate culture.

Leading with Compassion During Crisis

Firefighters regularly face traumatic events, such as fatalities, serious injuries, and life-threatening situations.

Compassionate leadership during these times is crucial. Leaders who provide emotional support, facilitate coping mechanisms, and lead with empathy during a crisis can help their personnel navigate the emotional aftermath.

- **Practical Strategies**: Fire service leaders can implement post-incident debriefings, offer grief support services, and ensure that personnel are not left to cope with traumatic events alone. Offering trauma-informed care and guidance will help personnel process difficult experiences and maintain their emotional well-being.

Compassion as a Cornerstone of Resilient Leadership

Compassionate leadership is essential for building a resilient fire service culture. By leading with empathy, understanding the emotional needs of personnel, and taking proactive steps to support mental health and well-being, leaders create an environment where firefighters can thrive, even in the most challenging circumstances. Compassion fosters trust, strengthens relationships, and enhances the overall effectiveness of the organization.

When leaders prioritize compassion, they cultivate a culture where individuals feel supported, valued, and empowered to handle the unique challenges of the fire service. A compassionate leader not only strengthens the resilience of their team but also sets the stage for long-term success in both personal and professional spheres.

CHAPTER TWENTY

Building Trust Through Transparent Communication

Chapter 20: Building Trust Through Transparent Communication

The Foundation of Effective Leadership

Effective leadership in the fire service is built on many pillars, but trust is the cornerstone of any strong team. Without trust, communication breaks down, morale diminishes, and the organization becomes vulnerable to dysfunction. One of the most powerful tools in building and maintaining trust is transparent communication. When leaders communicate openly and honestly with their teams, it fosters a culture of mutual respect and accountability.

Transparent communication means sharing information clearly, timely, and honestly. It requires leaders to be open about the challenges the organization faces, the decisions that need to be made, and the expectations for the team. In the high-stakes environment of the fire service, where split-second decisions can mean the difference between life and death, transparency is essential for ensuring that every member of the team is aligned and ready to act when needed.

The Importance of Transparency in Leadership

Trust in leadership is not something that can be assumed; it must be earned and cultivated over time. Transparency is one of the key behaviors that helps leaders earn that trust. When leaders are open with their teams, they demonstrate honesty, integrity, and vulnerability. These actions convey to team members that their leaders value them and believe in their ability to contribute to the organization's success.

Why Transparency Matters

Transparency helps remove uncertainty and ambiguity. When team members are kept in the loop about organizational goals, challenges, and changes, they feel more secure in their roles. This sense of security is vital in high-stress professions like the fire service, where employees are constantly faced with potentially dangerous situations.

- **Practical Strategies**: Leaders can promote transparency by regularly updating their teams on organizational goals, changes in policies, or other important developments. This can be done through regular meetings, newsletters, or team huddles to keep everyone informed and aligned.

The Role of Consistency in Transparent Communication

Transparency does not only occur in isolated instances; it must be consistent. Leaders who practice transparent communication on a regular basis show their team that honesty is not situational or selective. Consistency in transparency builds trust over time, while sporadic or selective transparency can lead to confusion, suspicion, and disengagement.

- **Practical Strategies**: Leaders should establish regular communication channels to ensure that transparency is consistent. For example, regularly scheduled briefings or meetings can provide the opportunity to communicate openly about ongoing projects, safety concerns, or the challenges the organization faces.

Open Lines of Communication: Encouraging Two-Way Dialogue

While transparency often focuses on the information provided by leaders to their teams, it is equally important to foster a two-way communication process. A leader who is truly transparent also actively listens to feedback, concerns, and ideas from their team. This reciprocal flow of information strengthens the relationship between leaders and their personnel and ensures that everyone has a voice in the decision-making process.

Creating Opportunities for Feedback

Feedback is a vital component of transparent communication. When leaders encourage feedback, they demonstrate that they value their team's opinions and are open to constructive criticism. This not only helps improve the team's performance but also creates a sense of ownership and inclusion.

- **Practical Strategies**: Leaders can create formal and informal opportunities for feedback. These can include anonymous surveys, one-on-one check-ins, or team discussions where feedback is encouraged and valued. Acknowledging and acting on the feedback received shows that leaders are committed to improvement and care about their team's perspectives.

Active Listening: A Key Component of Two-Way Communication

Effective two-way communication requires active listening. Leaders must give their full attention to the person speaking, demonstrate empathy, and respond thoughtfully.

This not only builds trust but also fosters a sense of connection and respect between leaders and team members.

- **Practical Strategies**: Leaders should make time to listen to their personnel, avoid distractions, and ask follow-up questions to clarify understanding. This shows the team that their input is genuinely valued and that their opinions matter.

Addressing Difficult Conversations with Transparency

Not all communication is easy, and difficult conversations are an inevitable part of leadership. Whether discussing poor performance, addressing interpersonal conflicts, or delivering bad news, leaders must approach these conversations with transparency and empathy. A leader who can navigate difficult conversations with honesty and respect not only solves the immediate issue but also strengthens their relationship with their team.

Honest Conversations About Performance

When it comes to addressing performance issues, transparency is key. It's important for leaders to provide clear, constructive feedback that focuses on behaviors and outcomes, rather than personal criticism. Transparent communication in these conversations ensures that team members understand the expectations and what steps they can take to improve.

- **Practical Strategies**: Leaders should have regular performance reviews, where expectations are clearly outlined, and feedback is given in a timely, constructive manner. They should avoid surprises and ensure that team members are aware of any areas that need improvement before formal evaluations take place.

Delivering Bad News with Empathy

Delivering bad news is never easy, but it's a necessary skill for leaders. Whether it's informing a team member about a termination, organizational restructuring, or an injury, leaders must handle these situations with transparency and empathy. Transparency in these conversations builds trust, as it shows that the leader is not hiding important information.

- **Practical Strategies**: When delivering bad news, leaders should provide clear explanations of the situation, the reasons behind the decision, and any actions that will follow. They should also offer support and be open to any questions or concerns the team member may have.

Transparency in Crisis Situations

In high-pressure situations, such as emergencies, fires, or critical incidents, transparent communication is crucial. In these moments, confusion and uncertainty can create panic, and clear, open communication can provide the stability needed to navigate the crisis. Leaders who maintain transparency during a crisis reassure their team, providing them with the confidence and information they need to act swiftly and decisively.

Maintaining Calm and Clarity

In chaotic situations, clear and transparent communication can prevent mistakes, reduce anxiety, and improve decision-making. Leaders should focus on providing clear, concise instructions and ensuring that their team understands their roles and responsibilities.

- **Practical Strategies**: During a crisis, leaders should give direct orders, ensure that all personnel are on the same page, and provide updates as the situation evolves. It's essential that the team feels informed and reassured, knowing that their leader is leading with clarity and transparency.

Supporting Personnel After the Crisis

After a crisis or critical incident, transparent

communication continues to play a vital role. It's essential for leaders to debrief the team, provide updates on the aftermath, and offer support to any individuals affected by the incident. This not only aids in the recovery process but also shows the team that their well-being is a priority.

- **Practical Strategies**: Leaders should facilitate post-incident debriefings, where they discuss what went well, what could be improved, and any lessons learned. Additionally, providing access to counseling or mental health support following a crisis is an important step in fostering a transparent, supportive environment.

Building Lasting Trust Through Transparent Leadership

Transparent communication is not just a leadership strategy; it's a foundational principle that can transform an organization. Leaders who communicate openly, listen actively, and address difficult conversations with honesty and empathy create a culture of trust, respect, and accountability. In the fire service, where lives are at stake, transparent communication is essential for fostering a resilient, cohesive, and effective team.

By embracing transparency, leaders can build strong,

trusting relationships with their personnel, ensuring that the team remains unified and focused, even during the most challenging times. Trust, once earned, becomes the glue that holds the team together, allowing them to face adversity with confidence and resilience.

B.R.I.C.K. BY B.R.I.C.K.

CHAPTER TWENTY-ONE

Embracing Adaptability and Change

Chapter 21: Embracing Adaptability and Change

The Unavoidable Nature of Change

In the fast-paced world of fire service leadership, change is the only constant. Whether it's advancements in technology, shifts in organizational priorities, or new challenges that emerge in the line of duty, adaptability is a critical skill for both leaders and their teams. Firefighters are routinely required to adapt to new situations, environments, and tactics to ensure the safety of themselves and the public. Leaders in the fire service must model this adaptability and guide their teams through the challenges that change brings.

Adaptability is the ability to adjust to new conditions, stay open to new ideas, and find solutions in situations that may initially seem insurmountable. The fire service is unique in that it demands adaptability not only in how it responds to emergencies but also in its organizational approach. Leaders who fail to embrace change or who resist new ideas risk hindering the growth and effectiveness of their team. On the other hand, leaders who embrace adaptability foster an environment where innovation thrives, and challenges become opportunities for improvement.

The Need for Adaptability in Fire Service Leadership

The fire service is an ever-evolving environment, and leadership must be flexible to respond effectively to changes. Whether these changes are driven by new fire safety regulations, emerging technologies, or evolving community needs, leaders must demonstrate the ability to adjust course and ensure their teams remain effective in dynamic situations.

Understanding the Forces of Change

Change within fire service organizations can come from a variety of sources: external pressures (e.g., public expectations, policy changes, budget constraints), internal factors (e.g., leadership changes, restructuring, personnel turnover), or technological advancements (e.g., new equipment, training methods, or communication systems). Leaders must stay attuned to these forces of change and make proactive adjustments to ensure their team is prepared to meet evolving challenges.

- **Practical Strategies**: To stay ahead of change, fire

service leaders should foster a culture of continuous learning and professional development. This can include regular training sessions, staying updated on industry trends, and encouraging feedback from team members about improvements that could be made to existing practices.

Leading by Example: Role of the Adaptable Leader

Adaptability in leadership is not just about responding to change, but also about setting the tone for the entire team. Leaders must demonstrate flexibility and openness to new approaches, showing their teams that change is not something to fear but something to embrace. When leaders model adaptability, their teams are more likely to follow suit and adopt a similar mindset.

- **Practical Strategies**: Leaders can model adaptability by demonstrating willingness to try new methods, seek feedback from their team, and adjust strategies based on the needs of the situation. Celebrating successful changes or adaptations can help reinforce the idea that change leads to growth.

Embracing Change to Improve Firefighting Practices

Change in firefighting tactics, equipment, and procedures

can often be met with resistance, especially when long-established methods have been effective in the past. However, failing to adapt to new innovations can leave teams vulnerable to outdated practices that no longer serve the best interests of public safety. Embracing change can lead to more effective firefighting strategies, enhanced safety measures, and better overall outcomes.

New Technologies and Equipment

Technological advancements are revolutionizing the way fire services operate, from the introduction of drones for aerial surveillance to the use of advanced thermal imaging cameras for locating victims in fires. Leaders who embrace these innovations can enhance the capabilities of their team, improving safety and operational efficiency.

- **Practical Strategies**: Leaders should facilitate the integration of new technologies by providing training and support for their team. Rather than resisting change, they should encourage their team to explore new tools and incorporate them into their everyday practices. This helps prevent complacency and opens the door to greater efficiency and effectiveness.

Revising Training and Tactics

Firefighting is an evolving discipline, and what worked a

decade ago may no longer be the most effective approach today. Leaders must regularly assess training programs, ensure they align with current best practices, and adapt them to meet the changing needs of the fire service. This might include adopting new techniques, revising safety protocols, or focusing on new types of training (e.g., stress management, leadership development, or diversity training).

- **Practical Strategies**: Leaders can implement regular assessments of training programs and procedures to ensure they remain relevant. This can involve feedback from team members on what works well, as well as attending industry conferences to stay up to date on the latest techniques and trends.

Overcoming Resistance to Change

Resistance to change is a natural human reaction, especially in environments where traditions are strong, and the consequences of mistakes can be severe. In the fire service, where many procedures are tested and time-honored, it's understandable that change may be met with skepticism. However, the inability to adapt can prevent progress and inhibit the team's ability to respond effectively to evolving needs.

Identifying Sources of Resistance

Resistance to change can stem from many factors: fear of the unknown, discomfort with new technologies, a sense of loss (e.g., losing established ways of doing things), or a lack of trust in leadership. Understanding the sources of resistance is the first step in overcoming it.

- **Practical Strategies**: Leaders should identify and address concerns early on by creating open channels for discussion. By acknowledging the source of resistance and offering support or clarification, leaders can ease the transition process and help their team embrace change with confidence.

Communicating the Why of Change

One of the most effective ways to overcome resistance to change is by clearly communicating the reasons behind it. When people understand the rationale for change—whether it's improving safety, enhancing efficiency, or meeting new regulations—they are more likely to accept it.

- **Practical Strategies**: Leaders should explain not only what is changing, but also why it's important. This transparency helps team members understand the bigger picture and their role in implementing the change. Providing a vision of the benefits of change can inspire motivation and reduce resistance.

Adaptability in Crisis Situations

The nature of the fire service means that change can happen in an instant. Whether it's a sudden shift in weather conditions, an unexpected technical failure, or a new safety protocol, fire service leaders must be prepared to adapt quickly in crisis situations. Their ability to remain calm, assess the situation, and adjust their approach can determine the outcome of the response.

Leading Through Uncertainty

During a crisis, adaptability is tested. Leaders must be able to think on their feet, adjust strategies in real-time, and remain focused on the mission at hand. They must also be able to manage the stress and uncertainty that comes with high-pressure situations while providing a clear, steady presence for their team.

- **Practical Strategies**: In crisis situations, leaders should encourage flexible thinking and empower their team to make decisions within the framework of safety and protocol. This encourages a culture of adaptability where team members are comfortable making adjustments as needed.

Learning from Crisis

Every crisis offers valuable lessons about what worked and what didn't. Embracing adaptability means taking the opportunity to learn from each situation, refining strategies, and continuously improving performance.

- **Practical Strategies**: After a crisis, leaders should facilitate debriefings where the team can discuss what happened, what could have been done differently, and what changes should be implemented moving forward. This continuous learning loop strengthens adaptability and improves future performance.

Adaptability as a Key to Long-Term Success

In the fire service, the ability to embrace adaptability and change is not just about surviving—it's about thriving. Leaders who foster adaptability in their teams can create an environment where challenges are met with innovation, and setbacks become opportunities for growth. By embracing change, fire service leaders can position their teams for long-term success, ensuring that they are prepared to meet the ever-evolving demands of their profession.

Change will always be part of the fire service, and those

who can adapt will be the ones to lead the way. By modeling adaptability, communicating the reasons for change, and supporting their teams through transitions, leaders can build resilient, high-performing teams capable of overcoming any challenge.

B.R.I.C.K. BY B.R.I.C.K.

CHAPTER TWENTY-TWO

Supporting Mental Health and Well-Being in the Fire Service

Chapter 22: Supporting Mental Health and Well-Being in the Fire Service

The Silent Struggles of First Responders

Firefighters, paramedics, and other first responders are regularly exposed to traumatic events that can take a significant toll on their mental health. From witnessing loss and suffering to dealing with the physical and emotional strain of high-pressure situations, the fire service is one of the most demanding professions, both mentally and physically. Yet, the culture of the fire service often emphasizes toughness and resilience, leading many to ignore or suppress the impact of stress and trauma. As a result, the mental health struggles of firefighters can often go unnoticed until they reach a crisis point.

This chapter will explore how fire service leaders can better support mental health and well-being within their teams, emphasizing the importance of creating an environment that encourages openness, provides resources for support, and promotes a culture of mental wellness.

Understanding the Mental Health Challenges in the Fire Service

The mental health challenges faced by firefighters are unique and can manifest in various ways. The nature of their work, combined with the cumulative stress of repeated exposure to traumatic events, can lead to conditions such as post-traumatic stress disorder (PTSD), anxiety, depression, and burnout.

Trauma Exposure and Its Impact

Firefighters are often the first responders to the most traumatic situations—fires, car accidents, medical emergencies, and violent incidents. Repeated exposure to such high-stress events can accumulate over time, leading to emotional exhaustion and psychological distress. The constant adrenaline rush, while initially energizing, can eventually lead to burnout if not managed properly.

- **Practical Strategies**: Leaders must encourage their team members to acknowledge the emotional toll of their work and provide regular opportunities for debriefing after traumatic events. This may involve peer support groups, counseling, or access to mental health professionals who specialize in trauma.

The Stigma Around Mental Health

One of the most significant barriers to addressing mental health in the fire service is the stigma that surrounds it. Firefighters often feel pressured to appear strong and resilient, fearing that seeking help for mental health concerns will be seen as a sign of weakness or inability to perform their duties. This stigma can prevent individuals from reaching out for the support they need, leading to the escalation of mental health issues over time.

- **Practical Strategies**: Leaders should actively work to normalize mental health discussions within the fire service. This includes openly discussing the importance of mental well-being and breaking down the barriers that prevent individuals from seeking help. Providing anonymous resources and ensuring confidentiality can also help remove the stigma associated with seeking mental health support.

Building a Culture of Mental Wellness

Creating a culture that values mental health and well-being is essential for long-term success in the fire service. This culture shift begins with leadership, as leaders must model and prioritize mental health in the same way they do physical health and safety.

Prioritizing Mental Health Training

Just as firefighters are trained in physical health and safety protocols, mental health training should be an integral part of their development. Training can include identifying signs of mental health struggles in oneself and others, learning coping strategies, and understanding available mental health resources.

- **Practical Strategies**: Leaders should incorporate mental health training into regular continuing education programs. This training should be interactive and involve scenario-based exercises where firefighters can practice responding to mental health issues, both in themselves and their peers.

Encouraging Open Communication

For mental health issues to be addressed effectively, there must be an open line of communication. Firefighters should feel comfortable discussing their emotional and psychological struggles without fear of judgment or retribution. This can be achieved through regular team check-ins, peer support groups, or one-on-one sessions with supervisors or counselors.

- **Practical Strategies**: Leaders can create opportunities for open communication by holding regular team meetings where mental health is discussed as part of overall well-being. These sessions should be safe spaces where employees can share their concerns and seek guidance without fear of stigma.

Implementing Support Systems

Having support systems in place is vital to ensuring that firefighters receive the help they need when they face mental health challenges. Support can come in many forms—peer support, professional counseling, critical incident stress management, and wellness programs.

Peer Support Programs

Peer support programs can be incredibly effective in providing emotional support to firefighters. These programs pair individuals who have experienced similar stressors to offer each other guidance, empathy, and encouragement. Peer supporters often provide a sense of solidarity and understanding that professional counselors may not be able to offer, as they have firsthand knowledge of the stresses of the job.

- **Practical Strategies**: Leaders should develop and promote peer support programs within their departments. This can involve training a group of firefighters to become peer supporters and ensuring they are equipped with the skills to listen, provide comfort, and refer peers to professional help if necessary.

Professional Mental Health Resources

Access to professional counseling services is essential for firefighters who are dealing with more severe mental health issues, such as PTSD or anxiety. Fire service leaders should ensure that their teams have access to qualified mental health professionals who specialize in trauma and the unique challenges of first responders.

- **Practical Strategies**: Leaders can partner with mental health organizations that specialize in first responder care to offer confidential counseling services. Additionally, they should create a system for ensuring easy access to these services, such as through an employee assistance program (EAP) or mental health hotline.

Preventing Burnout: Self-Care and Resilience

Preventing burnout is another crucial aspect of supporting mental health in the fire service. Burnout occurs when the emotional and physical demands of the job outweigh the individual's capacity to cope. It can lead to exhaustion, disengagement, and reduced job satisfaction.

Encouraging Resilience

Resilience is the ability to bounce back from adversity. Building resilience involves teaching firefighters effective coping strategies, stress management techniques, and the importance of rest and recovery. Resilient individuals are more likely to maintain their mental health, even in the face of stress and trauma.

- **Practical Strategies**: Leaders can encourage resilience by promoting stress-relief activities such as physical exercise, mindfulness, meditation, and hobbies. Providing time for adequate rest, ensuring work-life balance, and encouraging participation in resilience-building workshops can further support firefighters' ability to cope with stress.

The Role of Leadership in Preventing Burnout

Leaders must actively work to prevent burnout by creating a healthy work environment that emphasizes balance, support, and proper self-care. This includes recognizing the signs of burnout in team members and taking appropriate steps to address it before it escalates into a crisis.

- **Practical Strategies**: Leaders should monitor their

team's workload and ensure that they are not being overworked. They should also provide opportunities for downtime, encourage vacations, and foster an environment that supports mental and physical recovery.

The Importance of Mental Health Support

Supporting mental health in the fire service is not just a matter of offering resources—it is about creating a culture where mental well-being is valued and prioritized alongside physical health and safety. By embracing mental health support, leaders not only improve the well-being of their team but also enhance the overall effectiveness and morale of the organization.

When leaders take action to provide the necessary support and foster open communication, they help break down the stigma surrounding mental health and ensure that firefighters are equipped to face both the physical and emotional challenges of their profession. By investing in mental health, fire service leaders are investing in the long-term success of their teams, fostering a healthier, more resilient workforce that can effectively meet the demands of their critical work.

CHAPTER TWENTY-THREE

Fostering a Positive Work Environment

Chapter 23: Fostering a Positive Work Environment

The Role of Environment in Mental Health and Performance

A positive work environment is crucial for the mental well-being of all employees, particularly those in high-stress professions like firefighting. In the fire service, the work environment isn't just about the physical surroundings—it encompasses the culture, communication, leadership style, and interpersonal relationships that define the day-to-day experience of firefighters. A supportive, inclusive, and respectful environment promotes mental health, reduces stress, and enhances performance.

This chapter will explore the elements of a positive work environment and how leaders can foster such an environment within the fire service. By addressing culture, communication, and leadership, fire service leaders can create a space where firefighters feel valued, supported, and motivated to perform at their best.

Understanding the Elements of a Positive Work Environment

A positive work environment consists of several key elements that contribute to both employee well-being and job satisfaction. These elements include healthy relationships, clear communication, mutual respect, and a focus on well-being.

Healthy Relationships

Strong, supportive relationships between colleagues are essential for building a positive work environment. In the fire service, where teamwork is critical to success, mutual respect and trust between team members create a foundation for collaboration and effectiveness. When firefighters feel supported by their peers, they are more likely to succeed in high-pressure situations.

- **Practical Strategies**: Leaders should encourage team-building activities that strengthen bonds among colleagues. Additionally, promoting a culture of inclusivity and respect ensures that all members feel valued and heard.

Clear and Open Communication

Communication is the backbone of any successful team. In the fire service, clear communication can be the difference between life and death. But beyond operational communication, leaders should prioritize open dialogue about concerns, goals, and feedback. An environment where feedback is welcomed and acted upon ensures that employees feel involved and respected.

- **Practical Strategies**: Leaders should establish regular channels for open communication, such as weekly check-ins or anonymous feedback systems. They should also encourage active listening and ensure that all team members have an opportunity to voice their thoughts and ideas.

Respect and Recognition

When employees feel respected and appreciated, their motivation and job satisfaction increase. In the fire service, where the work is physically demanding and emotionally taxing, it is especially important for leaders to recognize the efforts and contributions of their team members. Recognition can come in many forms—whether through a formal award system or simple acknowledgment in daily interactions.

- **Practical Strategies**: Leaders should make it a priority to regularly recognize the hard work and dedication of their teams. This can include both formal recognition programs and informal praise during team meetings or one-on-one sessions.

Leadership's Role in Shaping the Work Environment

Leaders have the greatest influence over the work environment. Their behavior, attitudes, and communication style set the tone for the entire team. A positive work environment begins with strong, compassionate leadership that values the well-being of its employees and fosters a culture of mutual respect and trust.

Leading by Example

Effective leaders lead by example. They model the behavior they expect from their team members, demonstrating integrity, respect, and dedication. When leaders show care for the well-being of their team, they inspire others to do the same. Leading by example also means being transparent, approachable, and accountable for one's actions.

- **Practical Strategies**: Leaders should take the time to connect with their team on a personal level, show empathy, and provide consistent support. This can involve participating in team-building activities, addressing concerns directly, and ensuring a fair and transparent decision-making process.

Encouraging a Culture of Feedback

Constructive feedback is essential for growth and development. However, feedback should be delivered in a way that is supportive and constructive, rather than critical or punitive. Leaders should encourage a feedback culture where both positive and constructive feedback are normalized, helping employees understand what they are doing well and where they can improve.

- **Practical Strategies**: Leaders can schedule regular one-on-one feedback sessions with their team members. These sessions should focus on both strengths and areas for improvement, ensuring that feedback is actionable and motivating. Additionally, leaders should create an environment where team members feel comfortable giving feedback to one another.

Addressing and Preventing Toxicity in the Fire Service

Toxic work environments are detrimental to both individual mental health and organizational success. In the fire service, a toxic environment can arise from issues like poor leadership, lack of trust, favoritism, bullying, or inadequate communication. When left unchecked, toxicity can lead to high turnover, burnout, and decreased morale.

Identifying Toxic Behaviors

Toxic behaviors often manifest in subtle ways but can have a profound impact on the overall work environment. These behaviors might include gossip, exclusion, negative attitudes, or a lack of accountability. Leaders need to be vigilant in identifying these behaviors early and addressing them before they spread and cause harm.

- **Practical Strategies**: Leaders should actively monitor the team dynamic and address any signs of toxicity immediately. This includes calling out negative behavior in a constructive way, providing training on respectful communication, and offering mediation for conflicts that may arise.

Promoting Respectful Behavior

Respect is the foundation of a positive work environment. Leaders must set clear expectations for respectful behavior and hold everyone accountable for maintaining these standards. This includes not only being respectful to peers but also to subordinates, superiors, and the community they serve.

- **Practical Strategies**: Leaders should implement a zero-tolerance policy for bullying or disrespectful behavior. Encouraging open discussions about respect and its importance can also help reinforce these values throughout the organization.

Creating a Work-Life Balance

The fire service can be demanding, but it is important for employees to have a healthy work-life balance. Without adequate time to rest and recharge, firefighters are more likely to experience burnout, stress, and other mental health issues. A positive work environment promotes balance by allowing time for recovery and encouraging employees to maintain their personal lives outside of work.

Scheduling and Time Off

Providing adequate time off and ensuring fair and manageable schedules are critical in supporting a healthy work-life balance. Leaders should recognize the importance of downtime and ensure that their teams have the opportunity to rest and recharge.

- **Practical Strategies**: Leaders can implement flexible scheduling options and ensure that all team members are able to take their vacations and personal time. They should also monitor workloads to ensure no one is overwhelmed or working excessive overtime.

Encouraging Personal Well-Being

Promoting personal well-being extends beyond physical health and includes mental, emotional, and social well-being. Encouraging employees to engage in activities that promote relaxation, hobbies, and family time helps foster a well-rounded, balanced life.

- **Practical Strategies**: Leaders should encourage participation in wellness programs, fitness activities, or stress-relief techniques. Providing resources for mental health, such as access to counseling or support groups, can also promote overall well-being.

The Power of a Positive Environment

A positive work environment is essential to the mental health and well-being of firefighters. It supports collaboration, reduces stress, increases morale, and ensures that individuals feel valued and respected. Leaders in the fire service must take an active role in creating and maintaining such an environment, as it is a key factor in both individual success and organizational effectiveness.

By fostering healthy relationships, clear communication, respect, and work-life balance, leaders can create an environment where firefighters thrive. Ultimately, a positive work environment contributes to a healthier workforce, better performance in high-stress situations, and a more resilient, supportive team.

B.R.I.C.K. BY B.R.I.C.K.

CHAPTER TWENTY-FOUR

Overcoming Burnout and Building Resilience

Chapter 24: Overcoming Burnout and Building Resilience

The Silent Threat of Burnout

Burnout is one of the most insidious and pervasive challenges faced by firefighters, especially in the high-pressure and emotionally taxing environment of fire service work. Defined as physical, emotional, and mental exhaustion caused by prolonged stress and workload, burnout not only impacts an individual's performance but also their overall well-being. For those in high-stakes roles like firefighting, the risk of burnout is significantly higher due to the unpredictable and often traumatic nature of the job.

This chapter will explore the signs and causes of burnout, strategies for overcoming it, and ways to build resilience to prevent it from occurring in the future. Leaders in the fire service play a pivotal role in recognizing burnout in their teams and fostering a culture of support, self-care, and mental health awareness.

Understanding Burnout: Signs and Causes

Burnout is not just about physical exhaustion—it's a complex, multi-dimensional condition that affects an individual's emotional, mental, and physical health. It can lead to a decrease in job performance, a lack of motivation, feelings of detachment, and a sense of helplessness. For many firefighters, burnout occurs after a prolonged period of exposure to high stress, trauma, or an overwhelming workload.

Signs of Burnout

It's important to recognize the signs of burnout early. Symptoms can appear gradually, and many individuals may not recognize them until they have reached a critical point. Some common signs of burnout include:

- **Emotional Exhaustion**: Feeling drained, overwhelmed, or mentally depleted, regardless of how much rest or sleep one gets.

- **Cynicism or Detachment**: Developing a negative or detached attitude toward the job, colleagues, or even the community served.

- **Reduced Performance**: A noticeable drop in work quality, productivity, and efficiency, despite continued effort.

- **Physical Symptoms**: Sleep disturbances, frequent illnesses, headaches, or other physical ailments that are often stress-related.

- **Increased Irritability**: Frustration, anger, or irritability with team members, family, or the community.

Causes of Burnout

Burnout is caused by a variety of factors, often linked to high levels of stress, poor work-life balance, and a lack of support. In the fire service, common causes of burnout include:

- **Chronic Stress**: Exposure to high-stress situations, such as life-threatening emergencies, trauma, and loss, over extended periods of time.

- **Unmanageable Workloads**: Overwork, long hours, and insufficient time for rest and recovery.

- **Lack of Control**: Feeling powerless or having little control over one's work environment or decision-making.

- **Insufficient Support**: Lack of emotional support, either from leadership or peers, or an absence of mental health resources.

- **Poor Leadership**: Toxic or unsupportive leadership can increase stress and contribute to feelings of helplessness and burnout.

Strategies for Overcoming Burnout

While burnout can feel overwhelming, it is possible to recover and regain a sense of balance. Overcoming burnout requires intentional effort, self-care, and often, external support.

Acknowledging and Accepting Burnout

The first step in overcoming burnout is acknowledging that it exists. Many individuals try to power through burnout, believing that they simply need to push harder. However, without addressing the underlying causes, this approach only prolongs the problem. Accepting that burnout is real and requires attention is crucial to recovery.

- **Practical Strategies**: Firefighters should be encouraged to assess their stress levels regularly and recognize early warning signs of burnout. Leaders can provide a safe space for individuals to share their struggles without fear of judgment.

Seeking Support

Support is essential in overcoming burnout. This can come in many forms, from peer support to professional counseling. Firefighters should be encouraged to reach out to trusted colleagues or mental health professionals when they feel overwhelmed. Leaders must also create a culture where seeking support is normalized, reducing the stigma surrounding mental health.

- **Practical Strategies**: Establish peer support programs, where experienced firefighters offer guidance and emotional support to those struggling with burnout. Encourage the use of Employee Assistance Programs (EAP) for counseling and mental health resources.

Rest and Recovery

Proper rest and recovery are vital to overcoming burnout. Firefighters often work long, irregular hours, but it is essential to make time for adequate sleep and downtime. Without proper rest, the body and mind cannot fully recover from the demands of the job.

- **Practical Strategies**: Fire service leaders can encourage balanced shift schedules and provide resources to ensure that firefighters take their necessary time off. Firefighters should also be taught the importance of sleep hygiene and relaxation techniques.

Setting Boundaries

Setting boundaries between work and personal life is a key strategy for preventing burnout. Firefighters often feel that they must be "on" at all times, but this constant state of readiness can lead to exhaustion. Learning how to say no and prioritize personal time is essential for long-term well-being.

- **Practical Strategies**: Leaders should model healthy boundaries by respecting the personal time of their team members. Firefighters should also be encouraged to disconnect from work-related communication during off-hours and focus on their personal lives.

Building Resilience: Preventing Future Burnout

Building resilience is about developing the ability to adapt and thrive in the face of adversity. Resilience helps firefighters manage stress, bounce back from setbacks, and prevent burnout before it takes root. Leaders can play an important role in fostering resilience by promoting a supportive, proactive approach to mental health.

Developing Emotional Resilience

Emotional resilience involves the ability to cope with stress and negative emotions in a healthy way. For firefighters, emotional resilience is essential when responding to traumatic events or high-pressure situations. Training in emotional regulation and mindfulness can help build resilience.

- **Practical Strategies**: Introduce resilience training programs that focus on stress management, mindfulness techniques, and emotional regulation. Encourage firefighters to engage in activities that promote emotional well-being, such as meditation, yoga, or journaling.

Creating a Supportive Culture

A supportive culture is key to resilience. When firefighters feel supported by their peers and leaders, they are more likely to recover from setbacks and remain mentally healthy. Leaders should actively work to create an environment where vulnerability and seeking help are viewed as strengths, not weaknesses.

- **Practical Strategies**: Foster a culture of openness and support by regularly checking in with team members, offering feedback, and encouraging team-building activities. Implement a buddy system for mental health support, where firefighters can lean on each other during difficult times.

Encouraging Continuous Learning

Continuous learning and professional development can help firefighters feel empowered and capable in their roles, which in turn helps build resilience. When individuals feel they are growing and developing in their profession, it reduces the feelings of stagnation and frustration that can contribute to burnout.

- **Practical Strategies**: Provide opportunities for skill-building, advanced training, and professional development. Encourage firefighters to pursue certifications and courses that enhance their expertise and confidence.

Resilience as a Lifelong Practice

Overcoming burnout and building resilience is not a one-time effort—it's a lifelong practice that requires ongoing attention and care. By recognizing the signs of burnout early, seeking support, and implementing strategies for recovery, firefighters can navigate the challenges of their profession without sacrificing their mental health. Additionally, fostering a culture of resilience within the fire service helps prevent burnout before it takes root, ensuring that firefighters can continue to serve their communities effectively and with mental well-being intact.

Leaders in the fire service must prioritize mental health and resilience-building efforts, recognizing that a resilient workforce is not only healthier but also more effective in responding to the challenges they face. Together, we can build a fire service culture where resilience is the foundation of both individual and organizational strength.

B.R.I.C.K. BY B.R.I.C.K.

CHAPTER TWENTY-FIVE

The Role of Leadership in Supporting Mental Health

Chapter 25: The Role of Leadership in Supporting Mental Health

Leadership and Its Impact on Mental Health

Leadership plays a critical role in shaping the mental health of a team, especially in high-pressure professions like the fire service. Leaders set the tone for the organizational culture, influencing how mental health is viewed, addressed, and prioritized. In the fire service, where personnel face frequent exposure to trauma, stress, and high-stakes decision-making, leadership can either foster resilience and mental well-being or contribute to further mental health challenges.

This chapter explores the vital role of leadership in supporting mental health within the fire service. It examines how effective leadership practices can prevent burnout, promote a culture of psychological safety, and create an environment where mental health is prioritized.

Understanding the Leadership-Mental Health Connection

Effective leadership is integral to the mental health of firefighters. The way leaders respond to stress, trauma, and mental health concerns can influence the overall mental well-being of their teams. Poor leadership, on the other hand, can exacerbate stress, cause confusion, and increase feelings of helplessness or burnout.

Leadership and Psychological Safety

Psychological safety refers to an environment where individuals feel safe to take risks, make mistakes, and share their concerns without fear of judgment or retribution. In the context of mental health, psychological safety is essential for firefighters to openly discuss their struggles, seek help, and take the necessary steps toward recovery without fear of stigma or discrimination.

- **Practical Strategies**: Leaders must cultivate an open-door policy where team members feel comfortable expressing their mental health challenges. Regular check-ins, anonymous feedback channels, and peer support systems can foster psychological safety.

The Role of Leadership in Reducing Stigma

One of the primary barriers to addressing mental health in the fire service is the stigma surrounding it. Firefighters, like many other first responders, may fear being labeled as weak or unfit for duty if they admit to struggling with mental health challenges. Leaders have the power to challenge these harmful stereotypes and create a culture where mental health is seen as an integral part of overall health.

- **Practical Strategies**: Leaders can set the example by discussing their own mental health openly, participating in mental health training, and encouraging team members to seek help when needed. Leadership should also ensure that mental health resources are easily accessible and that employees are aware of the available support options.

Leading by Example: Modeling Healthy Behaviors

Leaders influence their teams by modeling behaviors, attitudes, and values. When leaders prioritize their own mental health and well-being, they send a powerful message to their teams about the importance of self-care. Conversely, when leaders ignore their own mental health or exhibit unhealthy behaviors, they create an environment where mental health issues are downplayed or ignored.

Prioritizing Self-Care

Self-care is crucial for maintaining good mental health, yet it is often overlooked in high-pressure environments. Leaders should make self-care a priority, not only for themselves but for their teams as well. Demonstrating healthy habits, such as taking breaks, exercising, and seeking professional support when needed, can help normalize the practice of self-care within the organization.

- **Practical Strategies**: Leaders should set boundaries around work hours, encourage physical and mental health breaks, and model healthy work-life balance practices. This sets the standard for the entire team to follow.

Promoting Mental Health Awareness

Leaders should continuously promote mental health awareness, both within their teams and throughout the organization. This includes providing education on recognizing signs of stress, burnout, and trauma, as well as promoting available mental health resources.

- **Practical Strategies**: Implement regular mental health training sessions, workshops, and resources for firefighters. Encourage the integration of mental health topics into regular team meetings to normalize conversations about psychological well-being.

Building a Supportive Work Environment

Creating a supportive work environment is essential for promoting mental health. Leaders should work to reduce unnecessary stressors, create systems of support, and offer opportunities for personal and professional growth. A supportive environment helps firefighters feel valued, respected, and empowered, all of which contribute to better mental health outcomes.

Reducing Stress Through Organizational Practices

Excessive stress is a significant contributor to mental health challenges in the fire service. Leaders can take proactive steps to reduce unnecessary stress by providing adequate resources, ensuring clear communication, and offering manageable workloads.

- **Practical Strategies**: Streamline administrative processes, provide adequate staffing levels, and ensure that firefighters have the necessary tools and training to do their jobs effectively. Open communication channels should be established to ensure that team members feel informed and involved in decision-making.

Fostering Peer Support

Peer support is a powerful tool in promoting mental health and resilience. Firefighters often turn to their colleagues for emotional support, as they share similar experiences and understand the unique challenges of the profession. Leaders can encourage and formalize peer support systems within their teams.

- **Practical Strategies**: Establish peer support programs where firefighters can confidentially discuss their mental health challenges with trusted colleagues. Training peer supporters can help ensure that these conversations are constructive and beneficial.

Creating Opportunities for Team Bonding

Strong team relationships can serve as a buffer against the stresses of the job. When firefighters feel a sense of camaraderie and trust with their colleagues, they are more likely to seek help when needed and experience a sense of emotional safety.

- **Practical Strategies**: Organize team-building exercises, social events, and collaborative projects to foster positive relationships among team members. Regularly engage in team check-ins to strengthen bonds and ensure that individuals feel supported by their peers.

Supporting Mental Health through Policies and Resources

Leaders must ensure that their organizations have the necessary policies and resources in place to support mental health. This includes ensuring that mental health services are accessible, reducing barriers to seeking help, and integrating mental health into the overall culture of the fire service.

Access to Mental Health Services

Firefighters should have easy access to mental health services, whether through employee assistance programs (EAPs), counseling services, or peer support networks. Leaders should ensure that these services are well-publicized and accessible to all team members.

- **Practical Strategies**: Regularly promote available mental health resources, including counseling services and hotlines. Ensure that mental health services are confidential, convenient, and available at all times.

Creating Mental Health Policies

Policies related to mental health should be clearly communicated and integrated into organizational practices. This includes creating policies around stress management, mental health support, and accommodations for individuals dealing with mental health challenges.

- **Practical Strategies**: Develop and communicate clear mental health policies that encourage early intervention, provide support for those struggling with mental health issues, and ensure that no one is penalized for seeking help.

A Culture of Care and Support

Leaders in the fire service have the power to create a culture of care, where mental health is prioritized, and individuals feel supported in their personal and professional lives. By leading with empathy, promoting self-care, and ensuring access to resources, leaders can build a workforce that is not only resilient but also empowered to tackle the challenges of the job without sacrificing their well-being.

Supporting mental health is not just about providing resources—it's about changing the way mental health is viewed and ensuring that mental health is treated with the same importance as physical health. When leaders take responsibility for fostering a culture of support, they create a safer, healthier, and more effective fire service that benefits both the individuals and the communities they serve.

B.R.I.C.K. BY B.R.I.C.K.

CHAPTER TWENTY-SIX

Building Resilience in the Face of Crisis

Chapter 26: Building Resilience in the Face of Crisis

The Importance of Resilience in the Fire Service

Resilience is often defined as the ability to recover from adversity or adapt in the face of significant challenges. In the fire service, resilience is not just a personal trait—it's a collective necessity. Firefighters frequently encounter high-stress situations, including emergencies, trauma, and physical dangers. The ability to remain mentally strong, adapt to rapidly changing circumstances, and continue performing under pressure is critical for both individual and team success.

Building resilience in the face of crisis is not about avoiding stress or difficulty; it's about learning how to thrive despite it. This chapter will explore strategies that leaders can employ to build resilience within their teams, as well as how firefighters can develop personal resilience to navigate the demands of their profession.

Understanding Resilience and Its Role in the Fire Service

Resilience is a dynamic quality that allows individuals to adapt to stress, overcome adversity, and ultimately grow stronger from challenges. In the context of the fire service, resilience is essential for responding to the physical and emotional demands of the job. Firefighters often face life-or-death situations that can create significant stress and trauma, making resilience a cornerstone of mental health and well-being.

The Resilience Process

Resilience is not a static trait—it's an ongoing process of adaptation, growth, and learning. Firefighters must be equipped with the mental and emotional tools to cope with the demands of their work, from dealing with traumatic events to managing stress over the long term.

- **Practical Strategies**: Leaders should foster a growth mindset within their teams, encouraging individuals to view challenges as opportunities to build resilience. This includes focusing on personal development, learning from past experiences, and seeking continuous improvement.

The Impact of Resilience on Mental Health

Resilience plays a crucial role in safeguarding mental health. When firefighters are able to bounce back from setbacks, process stress effectively, and learn from adversity, they are better equipped to avoid the negative consequences of trauma, burnout, and mental health disorders such as PTSD and depression.

- **Practical Strategies**: Implement programs focused on mental health resilience, such as stress management workshops, mindfulness training, and techniques for emotional regulation. These programs can help individuals develop the tools to cope with the unique stresses of their role.

The Role of Leadership in Cultivating Resilience

Leaders are key in shaping an environment that fosters resilience. By providing support, resources, and guidance, leaders can help firefighters develop the mental fortitude needed to persevere through difficult situations. Strong leadership can enhance a team's ability to stay composed and resilient, even in the face of the most challenging circumstances.

Leading with Empathy and Understanding

Leaders who lead with empathy create a supportive and compassionate work environment, which is fundamental for building resilience. When firefighters feel understood, valued, and cared for, they are more likely to trust their leaders and their team, which increases their ability to cope with stress and adversity.

- **Practical Strategies**: Leaders should model empathetic behaviors by actively listening to their team members, acknowledging their struggles, and offering guidance and support when needed. Regular check-ins, open communication, and fostering a culture of mutual respect can help to strengthen relationships and resilience within the team.

Encouraging Self-Reflection and Personal Growth

Resilience is closely tied to personal growth. Encouraging firefighters to reflect on their experiences, both positive and negative, helps them process and learn from their challenges. Leaders who promote self-reflection encourage individuals to identify their strengths, weaknesses, and coping strategies, which can improve overall resilience.

- **Practical Strategies**: Incorporate opportunities for reflection into team meetings or training sessions.

Encourage individuals to share their experiences, discuss how they overcame obstacles, and brainstorm strategies for future challenges.

Building Collective Resilience: Teamwork and Cohesion

While personal resilience is vital, collective resilience within the team is equally important. In the fire service, teamwork is essential for handling crises effectively. Firefighters must rely on one another for support, communication, and problem-solving. When teams function cohesively, they can face even the most intense crises with confidence and adaptability.

The Power of Teamwork in Building Resilience

Firefighting is a team-based profession. The collective strength of a team often determines the success of their operations, especially in high-stress situations. Building team resilience requires fostering an environment where collaboration, trust, and shared responsibility are prioritized.

- **Practical Strategies**: Implement team-building exercises that focus on communication, trust-building, and problem-solving. Encourage teams to debrief after incidents to discuss what went well, what could be improved, and how to better support one another during future challenges.

The Role of Shared Responsibility in Resilience

When everyone on the team shares responsibility for the well-being of the group, resilience is naturally reinforced. This shared responsibility helps firefighters feel a sense of duty to one another, motivating them to support their colleagues and stay strong in difficult situations.

- **Practical Strategies**: Create a culture of shared accountability by assigning team roles that emphasize collaboration. Encourage team members to check in with each other regularly and provide emotional and physical support when needed.

Developing Personal Resilience: Individual Strategies

While leaders play a vital role in building resilience, individuals must also take proactive steps to develop their own mental and emotional strength. Firefighters can enhance their personal resilience through various coping strategies, self-care practices, and mental health techniques.

Developing Mental Flexibility

Resilient individuals are mentally flexible—they can adapt to changing circumstances, shift their mindset, and approach challenges from different angles. Mental flexibility allows firefighters to manage stress, remain focused on their tasks, and respond to crises with clarity and composure.

- **Practical Strategies**: Encourage mindfulness practices, such as meditation or deep breathing exercises, which help individuals cultivate mental flexibility. Incorporate stress-relief techniques into daily routines, such as visualization, journaling, or progressive muscle relaxation.

Building Emotional Resilience

Emotional resilience is the ability to manage and regulate emotions, even in high-stress situations. Firefighters must be able to stay calm and composed when responding to traumatic events, all while processing their own emotional reactions. Building emotional resilience involves developing the ability to recognize and manage emotions, as well as seeking support when needed.

- **Practical Strategies**: Promote emotional regulation techniques, such as emotional awareness, mindfulness, and cognitive reframing. Encourage firefighters to seek support from peers or mental health professionals when they experience intense emotions or struggle with stress.

Enhancing Physical Resilience

Physical resilience is closely linked to overall well-being and mental health. Firefighters who take care of their physical health—through exercise, nutrition, and rest—are better able to cope with the physical demands of their job and recover from stressful situations.

- **Practical Strategies**: Encourage physical fitness programs that are tailored to the specific demands of firefighting. Promote healthy eating habits, adequate sleep, and regular physical activity as part of overall resilience-building.

Resilience as a Lifelong Journey

Building resilience is not a one-time event; it is a lifelong process. Firefighters must continuously cultivate their resilience through self-awareness, personal growth, and ongoing support from their leaders and teams. By investing in resilience at every level—individual, team, and organizational—firefighters can develop the strength and mental fortitude needed to face the challenges of their profession.

Leaders in the fire service must understand that resilience is key to maintaining both mental and physical well-being. By providing the resources, support, and guidance necessary to develop resilience, leaders can help create a culture where firefighters can thrive in the face of crisis.

B.R.I.C.K. BY B.R.I.C.K.

CHAPTER TWENTY-SEVEN

The Importance of Psychological First Aid

Chapter 27: The Importance of Psychological First Aid

Understanding the Need for Psychological First Aid in the Fire Service

Psychological First Aid (PFA) is a crucial tool for supporting mental health during and after crises. Just as physical first aid is necessary for treating injuries, PFA helps address the emotional and psychological needs of individuals following traumatic events. For firefighters, who often face life-threatening situations and witness significant trauma, understanding and implementing PFA is essential for maintaining mental well-being.

This chapter explores the concept of Psychological First Aid, its application in the fire service, and how it can be integrated into daily operations to support firefighters' mental health. We will also examine how leaders can be proactive in fostering an environment where psychological support is prioritized and accessible to all team members.

What is Psychological First Aid?

Psychological First Aid is an evidence-informed approach designed to reduce the initial distress caused by traumatic events and to promote adaptive functioning. Unlike traditional mental health interventions, PFA focuses on providing immediate, practical support and stabilizing individuals in the aftermath of a crisis.

Core Components of Psychological First Aid

The main goal of PFA is to provide emotional support and help individuals feel safe, connected, and empowered. The core components of PFA include:

- **Establishing Safety**: Ensuring that individuals feel physically and emotionally safe.

- **Providing Comfort**: Offering reassurance and a sense of calm.

- **Stabilizing Emotional Responses**: Helping individuals manage overwhelming emotions such as fear, anger, or anxiety.

- **Assessing Needs**: Identifying individuals who may require further psychological support or specialized care.

- **Connecting to Resources**: Helping individuals

access mental health services, peer support, or other resources if needed.

The Role of Firefighters in Providing PFA

Firefighters are often on the front lines of emergencies, not only responding to physical crises but also being among the first to witness emotional and psychological distress. As a result, they play a critical role in providing initial psychological support to their peers, victims, and community members during high-stress situations.

- **Practical Strategies**: Firefighters should be trained to recognize signs of distress in themselves and others and be equipped with the tools to offer immediate emotional support. This includes learning how to listen actively, offer reassurance, and provide comfort during times of crisis.

Psychological First Aid for Firefighters: An Organizational Responsibility

While individual firefighters can provide immediate support, it is also the responsibility of fire service organizations to implement structured programs that emphasize psychological well-being. This chapter will outline how fire service leaders can foster a supportive environment and create systems to encourage the use of PFA both in the field and after the incident.

Creating a Culture of Psychological Safety

A critical first step in building psychological resilience within the fire service is creating a culture of psychological safety. This means normalizing conversations about mental health, reducing stigma, and encouraging openness and support around emotional well-being. Firefighters should feel comfortable seeking help when needed, without fear of judgment or career repercussions.

- **Practical Strategies**: Encourage regular discussions about mental health during training sessions or team meetings. Fire service leaders should set the tone by openly discussing their own mental health experiences and normalizing the need for psychological care.

Providing Training in Psychological First Aid

Firefighters and leaders alike should be trained in the principles and practices of PFA. This training helps ensure that team members are equipped with the necessary skills to offer support when traumatic events occur. Proper training in PFA can also help prevent the onset of long-term mental health issues by addressing distress early on.

- **Practical Strategies**: Implement regular training sessions focused on PFA, mental health first aid, and stress management. Training should also include how to identify warning signs of psychological distress, including burnout, PTSD, and depression.

Recognizing Signs of Psychological Distress

Being able to recognize the signs of psychological distress in oneself and others is a key component of PFA. Firefighters who are trained to identify these signs can intervene early and provide support before symptoms escalate into more serious mental health issues.

Early Signs of Psychological Distress

Signs of distress can vary widely, but common symptoms include:

- **Physical symptoms**: Fatigue, headaches, sleep disturbances, stomach issues.

- **Emotional symptoms**: Irritability, anxiety, sadness, withdrawal, emotional numbness.

- **Behavioral symptoms**: Changes in appetite, increased alcohol consumption, reckless behavior, and avoidance of situations.

- **Cognitive symptoms**: Difficulty concentrating, memory problems, confusion, intrusive thoughts.

Responding to Psychological Distress

Once signs of psychological distress are identified, it is essential to respond with compassion and appropriate action. Offering comfort, ensuring that individuals have the support they need, and guiding them toward professional care are all important steps.

- **Practical Strategies**: Encourage team members to approach their colleagues with empathy and understanding. When signs of distress are recognized, offer the person the option to talk, connect them with peer support, and, if necessary, refer them to mental health professionals for further assistance.

Implementing PFA During and After Incidents

In the fire service, PFA is needed not only during emergencies but also in the aftermath. The days and weeks following a traumatic incident can be a vulnerable time for firefighters and those they assist. Providing consistent psychological support and ensuring that individuals have access to resources is essential for long-term recovery.

Immediate PFA After an Incident

Immediately following an emergency, it is important to provide a supportive environment where individuals can process the emotional impact of the situation. This includes offering reassurance, providing emotional comfort, and helping individuals regain a sense of control over their emotions.

- **Practical Strategies**: After responding to a traumatic call, conduct a quick debriefing where team members can express their feelings, share experiences, and discuss their emotional reactions in a safe space. Encourage open communication and validate each person's response to the incident.

Long-Term Psychological Support

Ongoing psychological support is just as important as the immediate aftermath. Firefighters need continued access to resources that promote mental health, such as counseling, peer support, and mental health check-ins. Leaders should ensure that support systems remain available long after the crisis has passed.

- **Practical Strategies**: Establish a system for ongoing mental health check-ins, such as monthly mental health assessments or peer-led support groups. Encourage firefighters to attend counseling sessions or workshops that focus on emotional recovery and resilience.

Psychological First Aid as a Lifelong Skill

Psychological First Aid is an invaluable skill for firefighters, enabling them to support each other through crises and to address the mental and emotional challenges that come with their profession. By implementing PFA into everyday practice and creating an environment where mental health is prioritized, the fire service can improve its overall resilience and ensure that both individuals and teams thrive under pressure.

Leaders who foster a culture of psychological safety and resilience can help mitigate the long-term effects of trauma, reducing the risk of burnout, PTSD, and other mental health issues. The responsibility of providing psychological first aid does not rest solely on individuals—it must be a collective effort that involves the entire fire service community working together to maintain mental well-being.

CHAPTER TWENTY-EIGHT

The Need for Leadership and Support in Mental Health

Chapter 28: The Need for Leadership and Support in Mental Health

The Role of Leadership in Mental Health

Leadership within the fire service is not only about making decisions, managing teams, and ensuring operational success; it also includes safeguarding the mental well-being of every team member. The importance of strong leadership in promoting mental health cannot be overstated, as leaders influence the culture and values within the organization. In a high-stress profession like fire service, the mental health of team members directly affects both individual performance and overall organizational success.

This chapter explores the critical role leadership plays in supporting the mental health of firefighters and why prioritizing mental well-being must be at the core of leadership responsibilities. We will examine the steps leaders can take to create a supportive environment, encourage open dialogue about mental health, and ensure that appropriate resources are available for those in need.

Understanding the Mental Health Crisis in the Fire Service

Firefighters face a unique set of challenges that can significantly impact their mental health. Exposure to traumatic events, high-pressure situations, and the physical demands of the job contribute to mental health risks such as PTSD, anxiety, depression, and burnout. However, the fire service has often struggled with addressing these issues in a proactive, structured manner.

The Impact of Trauma on Firefighters

Firefighters regularly witness life-threatening situations and traumatic incidents, which can leave emotional scars. These experiences often go unaddressed, as the culture within many fire departments can discourage open discussions about mental health. The "tough it out" mentality, while built on resilience, can prevent individuals from seeking help when they need it most.

- **Practical Strategy**: Leaders must create an environment where vulnerability is not seen as a weakness. Firefighters need to feel supported and empowered to talk about their mental health without fear of stigma.

Burnout and the Mental Health Toll of Stress

The demanding nature of the job can lead to burnout, especially when there is inadequate support for stress management. Burnout in the fire service is not just about physical exhaustion but also emotional and mental depletion. Leaders must recognize the signs of burnout and intervene before it leads to long-term mental health problems.

- **Practical Strategy**: Leaders should regularly assess the emotional and psychological well-being of their teams. Encourage employees to take breaks, provide adequate recovery time after intense incidents, and ensure access to counseling or support groups.

The Role of Leadership in Promoting Mental Health

Effective leadership can transform the mental health landscape of an organization. By fostering a culture of care and supporting mental health initiatives, leaders can reduce the stigma surrounding mental health issues and increase the likelihood of early intervention. Strong leadership creates an environment where mental health is just as important as physical health.

Leading by Example

One of the most powerful ways a leader can promote mental health within the fire service is by leading by example. When leaders openly discuss mental health, seek help when needed, and prioritize their own well-being, they set a precedent for others to follow. This transparency helps break down barriers and encourages team members to seek support without fear of judgment.

- **Practical Strategy**: Leaders should share their personal experiences with mental health struggles and emphasize that taking care of one's mental health is a critical part of being an effective firefighter. This will create a more open and accepting environment where mental health is normalized.

Establishing Mental Health Policies

Leaders must advocate for the development and implementation of clear mental health policies within their organizations. This includes setting up confidential support systems, providing access to mental health resources, and ensuring that mental health is considered a priority alongside physical fitness.

- **Practical Strategy**: Develop and communicate a comprehensive mental health policy that outlines the available resources for employees, the steps to access support, and the importance of mental health in the organization's overall well-being.

Creating a Supportive Environment for Mental Health

A supportive work environment is essential for promoting mental health and resilience. Leaders must ensure that firefighters have access to the resources they need to maintain their mental health, including mental health days, peer support programs, and counseling services. Creating a psychologically safe environment allows firefighters to openly discuss their struggles and seek help when necessary.

Normalizing Mental Health Conversations

Stigma around mental health is still prevalent in many first responder communities. Leaders have the responsibility to challenge this stigma by fostering open, honest discussions about mental health. Regular discussions, workshops, and training sessions can help normalize these conversations and remind everyone that mental health is an ongoing priority.

- **Practical Strategy**: Implement regular training on mental health awareness and create a supportive peer network where firefighters can talk about their struggles with people who understand the unique challenges they face.

Providing Access to Resources

Providing easy access to mental health resources is one of the most important ways leaders can support their team members. Whether through Employee Assistance Programs (EAPs), counseling services, or peer support networks, leaders must ensure that mental health support is easily accessible and confidential.

- **Practical Strategy**: Partner with mental health professionals to offer workshops, counseling sessions, and crisis intervention resources. Consider having an in-house mental health professional or designated support team member to provide ongoing care and guidance.

Addressing the Specific Needs of Firefighters

Each individual in the fire service has unique mental health needs, and leadership must be responsive to these needs. Acknowledging the mental health challenges specific to the profession and providing tailored support helps build resilience among firefighters. Leaders who understand the nuanced psychological demands of the job can better address and support the emotional needs of their teams.

Tailoring Support to the Needs of Firefighters

Firefighters may experience different types of stress depending on their role, years of service, or the particular challenges they face in the field. Leaders must work to understand these unique experiences and provide support that is specifically tailored to the needs of their team.

- **Practical Strategy**: Create specialized programs that cater to the needs of different teams within the department. For instance, rescue teams may experience different psychological stress than those working in administrative or training roles. Provide resources and support based on specific needs and experiences.

Recognizing the Long-Term Effects of Stress

The impact of chronic stress and trauma in the fire service can be long-lasting, with cumulative effects on an individual's mental health. Leaders must recognize the signs of long-term stress and intervene early to prevent the development of more severe mental health issues.

- **Practical Strategy**: Implement regular check-ins, mental health screenings, and resilience training to monitor long-term effects. Offer mental health resources designed to prevent burnout and PTSD.

Transforming Mental Health Support Through Leadership

Leadership within the fire service has the power to transform the way mental health is perceived and managed. By leading with empathy, normalizing mental health conversations, and ensuring that appropriate resources are available, leaders can create a culture of care and resilience. When mental health is prioritized as part of the overall well-being of firefighters, they are more likely to succeed in their personal and professional lives.

The fire service community is built on trust, camaraderie, and teamwork. By supporting the mental health of team members, leaders not only enhance the well-being of individuals but also strengthen the entire organization. It is time for fire service leaders to step up and take responsibility for the mental health of their teams, ensuring that no firefighter has to face their challenges alone.

CHAPTER TWENTY-NINE

Building Resilience in Firefighters

Chapter 29: Building Resilience in Firefighters

The Importance of Resilience in the Fire Service

Resilience is one of the most vital qualities for anyone working in high-stress, high-risk environments, and nowhere is this more evident than in the fire service. Firefighters face trauma, long hours, physical and emotional strain, and moments of intense danger. Resilience—the ability to bounce back from these challenges and continue forward—is essential to their success and mental well-being.

In this chapter, we will explore how resilience is developed, how it can be supported within the fire service, and why it is a critical component of both individual and organizational success. We'll also examine the role of leadership in cultivating resilience and how this leads to long-term mental health and well-being for firefighters.

Defining Resilience in the Fire Service

Resilience is often described as the ability to "bounce back" after adversity. However, for firefighters, it goes beyond just recovery—it involves the mental fortitude to handle ongoing stress, adapt to changing environments, and continuously perform under pressure. Firefighters must not only recover from traumatic incidents but also learn how to thrive despite the difficulties they face.

The Key Components of Resilience

Resilience is not an inherent trait that some people are born with, but rather a skill that can be developed and strengthened over time. The key components of resilience in the fire service include:

- **Emotional Regulation**: The ability to manage emotions, especially in stressful or traumatic situations.

- **Optimism and Positivity**: Maintaining a hopeful outlook even in the face of challenges.

- **Problem-Solving Skills**: The ability to find solutions and take decisive action when facing obstacles.

- **Social Support**: Relying on colleagues, friends, and family for emotional support and guidance.

- **Self-Efficacy**: Believing in one's ability to handle challenges and succeed.

By focusing on these components, leaders can help firefighters develop the mental strength required to cope with the inherent stress of their work.

The Role of Leadership in Building Resilience

Leadership is instrumental in fostering an environment that encourages resilience. Leaders within the fire service can model resilience, provide support, and implement programs that build mental toughness and coping mechanisms for their teams.

Leading by Example

Firefighters often look to their leaders for guidance and inspiration. When leaders demonstrate resilience—by staying calm under pressure, maintaining a positive attitude, and taking proactive steps to manage stress—they set a powerful example for their teams. Resilient leadership encourages others to follow suit, creating a culture of resilience that is embedded within the organization.

- **Practical Strategy**: Leaders should prioritize their

own mental health and demonstrate self-care practices. When a leader takes time to engage in stress-reduction activities and seeks support when needed, it signals to the team that it is acceptable to do the same.

Providing Resources for Resilience Training

Training in resilience is as important as physical fitness training. Firefighters need skills to cope with the psychological demands of their work. This includes stress management techniques, mindfulness practices, emotional intelligence training, and building strong social support networks.

- **Practical Strategy**: Integrate resilience training into regular professional development. Offer workshops, seminars, and practical exercises focused on stress management, mental well-being, and coping skills. Consider bringing in mental health professionals or resilience coaches to conduct these sessions.

Building a Culture of Support

A supportive organizational culture is essential for resilience. When firefighters feel supported, both by their leadership and their peers, they are better equipped to handle the emotional and psychological stresses of the job.

Support can come in many forms—emotional, social, and professional—and must be woven into the fabric of the fire service.

Peer Support Programs

Peer support programs are one of the most effective ways to build resilience within the fire service. These programs allow firefighters to lean on their colleagues for support, share their experiences, and receive emotional guidance from people who understand the specific challenges of their profession. Peer support helps to destigmatize mental health challenges and fosters a sense of camaraderie and trust within teams.

- **Practical Strategy**: Develop a formal peer support program that includes training for peer supporters and clear procedures for how to access support. Encourage firefighters to speak openly about their mental health without fear of judgment.

Encouraging Social Connections

Social support is a cornerstone of resilience. Firefighters who have strong relationships with their colleagues, friends, and family are better able to manage stress and recover from traumatic events. Leaders should actively encourage social bonding, both within and outside of work, to help build these crucial connections.

- **Practical Strategy**: Organize social events, team-building activities, and off-duty support networks to strengthen bonds between colleagues. Creating a sense of community and mutual support improves resilience and reduces feelings of isolation.

Resilience in Action: Practical Strategies for Firefighters

Building resilience isn't just about theoretical concepts—it's about practical, day-to-day strategies that firefighters can use to maintain their mental well-being and perform at their best.

Stress Management Techniques

Firefighters must develop strategies to manage stress both on the job and in their personal lives. Techniques such as deep breathing, progressive muscle relaxation, meditation, and yoga can help reduce the impact of stress. Regular physical exercise is also vital for maintaining both physical and mental health.

- **Practical Strategy**: Encourage regular use of stress management tools during and after shifts. Provide access to relaxation spaces, mental health resources, and fitness programs to support stress relief.

Building Mental Toughness Through Reflection

Reflection is a powerful tool in building resilience. Firefighters can benefit from taking time to reflect on their experiences, both positive and negative. This reflection allows them to process difficult emotions, learn from challenges, and build a more resilient mindset.

- **Practical Strategy**: Encourage firefighters to engage in debriefing sessions after particularly challenging incidents. These sessions should provide a safe space for firefighters to reflect, share their feelings, and receive emotional support from their peers.

Resilience as a Foundation for Mental Health

Resilience is not just about surviving the fire service; it's about thriving despite the challenges. When resilience is cultivated and supported, firefighters can handle the stress, trauma, and emotional demands of their work without sacrificing their mental health. Strong, resilient teams lead to better outcomes not only for individuals but for the entire organization.

Leaders in the fire service play a pivotal role in fostering resilience by providing the resources, support, and training necessary to develop this crucial trait. When resilience is prioritized, it becomes a foundation upon which mental health, well-being, and organizational success are built.

CHAPTER THIRTY

The Path Forward — Resilience and Mental Health as an Ongoing Journey

Chapter 30: The Path Forward—Resilience and Mental Health as an Ongoing Journey

Embracing the Ongoing Nature of Mental Health and Resilience

In the fire service, as in any profession that involves high levels of stress and trauma, resilience and mental health are not static states—they are ongoing processes that require continual attention and care. This chapter will explore the necessity of sustaining resilience practices over the long term and the importance of viewing mental health as an evolving journey rather than a fixed destination.

Mental health and resilience are deeply intertwined. A resilient firefighter is better equipped to handle the psychological demands of the job, and by nurturing mental health, resilience becomes stronger over time. This chapter will focus on how organizations can create environments that promote both ongoing resilience and mental well-being for their personnel, ensuring that mental health is not only addressed when problems arise but is proactively supported throughout a firefighter's career.

Resilience is a Journey, Not a Destination

It is important to recognize that resilience is not a one-time achievement but an ongoing process that must be continuously nurtured. Like physical fitness, mental resilience requires regular attention, practice, and sometimes professional guidance.

The Dynamic Nature of Resilience

Resilience involves adapting to life's challenges, but it doesn't mean that individuals will be unaffected by adversity. Instead, resilient people can acknowledge their emotional responses, adjust to stressors, and continue forward. This ability must be developed over time, and maintaining it requires commitment to personal growth, mental health, and self-care practices.

- **Practical Strategy**: Encourage firefighters to view resilience as a lifelong journey. Promote activities that cultivate mental toughness, such as continuous learning, mindfulness practices, and building supportive relationships both in and outside of the fire service.

Ongoing Support and Mental Health Resources

Mental health challenges in the fire service are not limited to the initial stages of a career. In fact, they can grow and evolve as individuals face new challenges and experiences. To ensure the mental well-being of firefighters throughout their careers, continuous access to mental health resources is essential.

Creating a Culture of Mental Health Support

A culture that normalizes mental health support encourages firefighters to seek help when they need it without fear of judgment or stigma. Mental health resources should be as readily available as physical training programs, and leaders should actively promote the importance of maintaining mental well-being throughout a firefighter's career.

- **Practical Strategy**: Implement long-term access to mental health resources, including counseling services, employee assistance programs (EAPs), and stress management workshops. Encourage firefighters to check in regularly with mental health professionals as part of their routine professional development.

Continuous Training on Mental Health Awareness

Just as physical training is a routine part of the fire service, so too should be mental health education. Regular training that focuses on recognizing early signs of mental health challenges, understanding how to manage stress, and encouraging open communication can ensure that firefighters are always prepared to address their mental health needs.

- **Practical Strategy**: Incorporate mental health awareness training into the ongoing education curriculum. Offer refresher courses and workshops focused on recognizing stress and trauma symptoms, developing coping strategies, and understanding how mental health impacts performance and well-being.

The Role of Leadership in Sustaining Resilience

Leadership plays a vital role in maintaining resilience across the fire service. It is not only the responsibility of individual firefighters to nurture their own resilience but also the duty of leaders to create environments that foster continual growth, support, and mental wellness. Leaders who actively prioritize mental health send a powerful message to their teams that well-being is just as important as physical fitness and skill development.

Modeling Lifelong Resilience Practices

Leaders should model resilience by consistently engaging in self-care practices, seeking support when needed, and demonstrating vulnerability. This sets an example for their teams, showing that resilience is not about being invincible but about understanding and taking care of one's mental and emotional needs.

- **Practical Strategy**: Leaders should share their own resilience strategies with their teams, including how they manage stress, deal with setbacks, and maintain their mental health. Leading by example helps normalize these behaviors and encourages others to follow suit.

Creating Safe Spaces for Vulnerability

One of the most important ways leaders can support long-term resilience is by fostering a work environment where vulnerability is viewed as a strength rather than a weakness. By encouraging open communication about mental health challenges, leaders create safe spaces for firefighters to seek support without fear of reprisal or judgment.

- **Practical Strategy**: Establish confidential peer support systems where firefighters can share their experiences without fear of stigma. Ensure that leadership is visibly supportive of these programs and that all personnel are encouraged to utilize them regularly.

Resilience Beyond the Fire Service

While resilience is crucial within the fire service, it extends far beyond the job itself. Firefighters are multifaceted individuals with lives, families, and responsibilities outside of the firehouse. Their resilience must be supported in all aspects of their lives, and maintaining a healthy work-life balance is essential for sustaining long-term mental health.

Balancing Work and Personal Life

A significant challenge for firefighters is maintaining a balance between their high-intensity, demanding jobs and their personal lives. Without clear boundaries, work stress can overwhelm family life, and vice versa. Leaders and organizations must acknowledge the importance of personal time and encourage firefighters to take regular breaks and disconnect from work when off duty.

- **Practical Strategy**: Promote a healthy work-life balance by offering flexible schedules, encouraging time off, and providing family support programs. Recognize that personal well-being is integral to professional performance.

Building Community and Support Networks Outside of Work

Firefighters should be encouraged to develop strong support networks outside of the fire service. These relationships—whether with family, friends, or community groups—help maintain a sense of perspective and provide emotional outlets for stressors that are not work-related.

- **Practical Strategy**: Encourage firefighters to engage in community activities, hobbies, and social events that help them build personal relationships outside of the firehouse. Strong personal support systems contribute to a more resilient and mentally healthy workforce.

Moving Forward: A Commitment to Resilience and Mental Health

The path to maintaining resilience and mental health in the fire service is ongoing. It requires a culture of support, continuous learning, and a commitment to both individual and organizational well-being. Leaders, peers, and the organization as a whole must be invested in fostering resilience to ensure that firefighters are not only prepared for the immediate stresses of their job but are also supported in their long-term mental health journey.

A Call to Action for Leaders

Leaders must take the responsibility of ensuring that resilience and mental health are embedded within the organizational culture. This includes providing ongoing support, modeling resilience practices, and prioritizing mental health initiatives. By creating an environment where mental health is valued and resilience is nurtured, leaders ensure that their teams are prepared for the challenges they will face both today and in the future.

Resilience as the Foundation for Future Success

As the fire service continues to evolve, so too must our approach to mental health and resilience. By recognizing the importance of ongoing support, continuous education, and leadership involvement, the fire service can build a workforce that not only survives the challenges of the job but thrives in the face of adversity. Resilience is not a static trait, but a dynamic journey that demands commitment, support, and continual growth.

As we move forward, let us remember that resilience, mental health, and the overall well-being of our firefighters are not afterthoughts but essential components of a thriving, successful fire service.

CHAPTER THIRTY-ONE

EPILOGUE: The Legacy of Resilience and Leadership in the Fire Service

Epilogue: The Legacy of Resilience and Leadership in the Fire Service

Epilogue: The Wizard of Oz—The Final Journey Home

Just as Dorothy's path through Oz was filled with flying monkeys, wicked witches, and crossroads where decisions had to be made, the path through the fire service is often marked by chaos, conflict, and unexpected forks in the road. Yet, what this journey reveals—if we are willing to see it—is that every obstacle is an opportunity to build something stronger: resilience, insight, and the courage to lead.

Dorothy never realized that the power to return home—to wholeness—was within her all along. The Scarecrow, Tin Man, and Lion weren't just companions; they were mirrors reflecting the very strengths she already possessed: discernment, compassion, and bravery. Likewise, in the fire service, each individual carries these capacities. But without leaders who nurture them, without a culture that values kinship over command-and-control, those strengths lie dormant.

This book has explored how poor leadership—marked by ego, neglect, and dysfunction—breaks more than spirits. It breaks systems, relationships, and the very resilience that is vital to mental health. But when we lead with **kindness amid chaos**, when we build teams that foster **conflict-resolution through kinship**, we lay each brick with purpose. That is the blueprint for psychological safety. That is the Yellow Brick Road.

At the center of this transformation is the **D.O.G.**:

- **Determination** to challenge toxic norms and speak truth to power.

- The ability to recognize and push through **Obstacles** without becoming jaded or disengaged.

- And the relentless pursuit of **Goals** that are not only personal but communal—ensuring that no one is left behind on the journey.

Toto—small and seemingly insignificant—was the reason Dorothy even began her journey. Just like in our own lives, the seemingly "minor" responsibilities we carry (family, service, integrity) often become the very reasons we must press forward. They give us purpose, even when systems and supervisors fail us.

Leadership in the fire service must stop pretending to be the Wizard—shiny and loud but hollow behind the curtain. Instead, it must become Glenda: the guide who reveals the truth, empowers others, and encourages self-belief. Real leadership builds brick by brick: not with control, but with connection. Not with demands, but with development.

We must remember that **resilience is not resistance**. It's not the ability to bear pain in silence or carry more than one should. It is the capacity to bend without breaking, to rebuild after hardship, and to bring others along in that process. It is forged in adversity and sealed in kinship.

So, ask yourself:

What is the size of your D.O.G.? What drives you to keep walking, even when the road twists through burnout, politics, or neglect? And more importantly, what kind of leader will you be for the next person on the path?

Let us commit to building a fire service that is not powered by fear or tradition, but by **vision, values, and validation**. One where firefighters don't just survive shifts—but leave better, stronger, and whole. Where we are not defined by what we endure, but by what we transform. That is the future. That is the destination. And brick by brick, that is how we find our way home.

As we conclude this journey through the intersections of resilience, leadership, and mental health in the fire service, we are reminded that the work is never truly finished. Resilience is not a destination—it is an ongoing commitment, a constant recalibration, and a journey that unfolds with every decision made, every challenge faced, and every lesson learned.

The fire service, with its unique demands and risks, is a profession that requires more than just technical expertise; it demands emotional intelligence, mental fortitude, and above all, a commitment to the well-being of every individual within the organization. As we've seen throughout this book, the cost of neglecting mental health and failing to nurture resilience is far-reaching, affecting not only the individual firefighter but also the communities they serve and the organizations they represent.

However, as we've also explored, there is hope. Through proactive leadership, a culture of support, and a commitment to self-awareness and self-care, we can create a fire service that not only survives but thrives. A service where every firefighter feels valued, supported, and equipped to handle the challenges of the job, both on the fireground and in their personal lives.

The road to building a mentally resilient fire service is

paved with understanding, compassion, and accountability. It is the responsibility of leaders at every level to recognize the signs of burnout, trauma, and stress, and to provide the resources and support necessary for healing and growth. Equally, it is the duty of every firefighter to acknowledge the importance of their own mental health, to seek help when needed, and to support one another on this journey.

Looking ahead, we must continue to challenge the stigma that surrounds mental health in the fire service. We must foster an environment where seeking help is not a sign of weakness but a demonstration of strength. And we must ensure that every firefighter has the tools, resources, and support systems they need to navigate their careers with resilience, pride, and purpose.

As we move forward, let us remember that the fire service is not just a profession; it is a calling. It is a vocation that requires not only the physical strength to face danger but the mental fortitude to continue serving with compassion, dedication, and resilience. By prioritizing mental health and resilience, we not only honor the legacy of those who have come before us but also ensure the well-being of future generations of firefighters.

In the end, the strength of the fire service lies not just in the bravery of its personnel but in the resilience of its leaders and the unwavering commitment to the mental and emotional health of every individual within the organization. Let this be the legacy we leave behind: a fire service that stands as a beacon of resilience, mental health, and unwavering support for all those who serve.

CHAPTER THIRTY-TWO

To DO

Lead with Humanity, Not Just Hierarchy

- Titles don't build trust — **integrity does**.

- Leaders must show they care about their team's *well-being*, not just their performance.

- A simple "How are you really doing?" goes further than we think.

- Create an atmosphere where vulnerability is not punished, but protected.

Normalize the Conversation About Mental Health

- If we can talk about how to breach a structure, we can talk about how trauma breached our psyche.

- Host mental health debriefs after tough calls, not just operational critiques.

- Encourage peer support teams that are trained, confidential, and credible.

Redefine Strength

- Strength is not silence.

- Resilience is not repression.

- True strength is *seeking help when needed and giving it when possible*.

- Celebrate courage in counseling the same way we celebrate courage on the fireground.

Prioritize Psychological Safety

- Members should feel safe to speak without fear of ridicule or retaliation.

- This includes challenging unsafe practices, reporting misconduct, or admitting when they are struggling.

- **Culture starts at the top**, but accountability must live at every level.

Build Rituals of Kindness

- Make room for team check-ins. Share meals, not just tasks.

- Recognize milestones — promotions, retirements,

and recoveries.

- Give credit often. Gratitude is a mental health multiplier.

Resilience is a Team Sport

Brothers and sisters,
We can train for every scenario — high-rise fires, hazmat, wildland deployments — but if we don't prepare our minds, we'll never be ready for the battle inside.

Poor leadership creates cracks in our foundation. Intentional kindness builds us back — stronger and more connected.

Let us remember that resilience is not built overnight. It is laid down — **brick by brick** — in moments of chaos, and in gestures of kindness.

We owe it to each other. We owe it to the next generation. And we owe it to ourselves.

Pour into your potential. Sip. Set. Succeed.
Together — let's lead, heal, and rise.

www.ingramcontent.com/pod-product-compliance
Lightning Source LLC
Chambersburg PA
CBHW050339230426
43663CB00010B/1919